WIGGO
MARCO
ALBERTO

MIGUEL
EDDY
NIBALI
CAV   SUE

ON THE ROAD.

A Velodrome Book

First published in Great Britain in 2016 by

Velodrome Publishing
A Division of Casemate Publishers
10 Hythe Bridge Street
Oxford OX1 2EW, UK
and
1950 Lawrence Road, Havertown, PA 19083 USA

www.velodromepublishing.com

Rider images courtesy Offside and Getty Images

A catalogue record for this book is available from the British Library

ISBN 978-1-911162-01-8

Printed in China

To receive regular email updates on forthcoming Velodrome titles, news and reader offers, please email info@velodromepublishing.com with 'Velodrome Updates' in the subject field.

For a complete list of Velodrome Publishing titles, please contact:
CASEMATE PUBLISHERS (UK)
Telephone (01865) 241249
Fax (01865) 794449
Email: casemate-uk@casematepublishers.co.uk
www.casematepublishers.co.uk

CASEMATE PUBLISHERS (US)
Telephone (610) 853-9131
Fax (610) 853-9146
Email: casemate@casematepublishing.com
www.casematepublishing.com

RICHARD MITCHELSON'S

GRAND TOUR

A CYCLIST'S CHAIN-DRIVEN
INTERACTIVE ARTISTIC ADVENTURE

 velodrome.publishing

For Elli, Amelia and Nora

Getting a new sketch book is an odd experience. It sits there, blank, white, cold, looking at you. Waiting for you to make the first mark, not the defining mark, but a mark all the same. Something to start a journey that you're not sure where will end. What I suggest you do is take a pen, pencil, ink, paint or anything and make a mark in this book, without thinking about it. Don't let this book sit on a shelf. It wants you to scribble and use colour in it. If it's left on a shelf it will look down and weep papery tears on you. Be bold. Pop the kettle on, have a brew and stick some tunes on. Then enjoy letting your mind play its way through each page. Think. But not too much. Don't take this book seriously. It's daft. It's meant to stick a smile on your face in a quiet moment of the day, or on the loo. That's often a quiet place. Enjoy it. Bend the pages. Show your pals you see every day. Show your pals online you've never met. Now make that mark. This book wants you to.

Thanks

R x

THIS IS IT! ARE YOU READY? THE WINTER'S HARD MILES HAVE BEEN DONE AND YOU AND THE TEAM EVEN WENT AND LIVED ON THE SIDE OF A MOUNTAIN AWAY FROM FAMILY, FRIENDS, BEER, CAKE AND ALL SORTS OF NICE THINGS IN LIFE TO PREPARE FOR THIS SEASON'S GRAND TOURS. IT'S GOING TO BE TOUGH, VERY TOUGH. WE ALL HAVE BAD DAYS BUT HOPEFULLY WITH ALL THIS GRAFT AND THE BEST TEAM IN THE WORLD, YOU CAN MAKE YOUR MARK ON THE HISTORY OF CYCLING AND TAKE HOME ONE OF THE BIGGEST PRIZES THE SPORT HAS TO OFFER.

WE START OUR JOURNEY IN ITALY, MOVE ON TO FRANCE AND FINISH IN SPAIN. EACH PAGE OF THE BOOK WILL TEST YOUR CYCLING KNOWLEDGE AND PUSH YOU TO THE LIMIT CREATIVELY. GET THE PENS, PAINT, INKS AND STICKY BACK PLASTIC READY — YOU'RE GOING TO NEED THEM ALL. THIS IS IT. THE DIRECTEUR SPORTIF HAS YOUR NAME EAR-MARKED FOR GREATNESS. THE WORLD'S PRESS AWAITS AND THE FANS KNOW YOU CAN DO IT. PIN THAT NUMBER ON, CLIP IN AND

GO!

Take the world with you on your ride:

@rich_mitch
@velodromepub
#RichMichGrandTour

GIRO D'ITALIA

MAY. 21 STAGES. 3,500KM ISH.

OH NO. THE OFFICIAL THAT DECIDES THE GIRO ROUTE HAS GONE ON HOLIDAY...

PASSO DELLO STELVIO

PASSO GAVIA

TRE CIMA DI LAVAREDO

COLLE DELL'AGNELLO

COLLE DELLA LOMBARDA

MILAN

KEY

▷ PARTENZA

○ START TOWN

○ FINISH TOWN

○ REST DAY

| | | | | | | | INDIVIDUAL TIME TRIAL

■ ■ ■ ■ TEAM TIME TRIAL

SO PENS AT THE READY,
YOU NEED TO CREATE 21 STAGES,
2 REST DAYS AND EVERYTHING ELSE
THAT MAKES A GRAND TOUR, GRAND, AND
GREAT. QUICK, THE WORLD IS WAITING!

DRESS THE RIDER

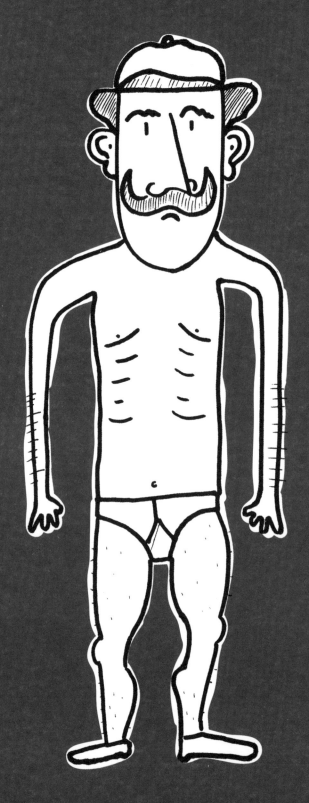

1900s

IT'S BREAKFAST, THE ROOM IS SILENT. THIS IS GOING TO BE A BIG STAGE FOR YOU AND THE TEAM... IT'S GOING TO BE BRUTAL. FILL YOUR PLATE READY FOR AN EPIC DAY AT THE OFFICE... GO BIG.

THE VELODROME
FIASCO.

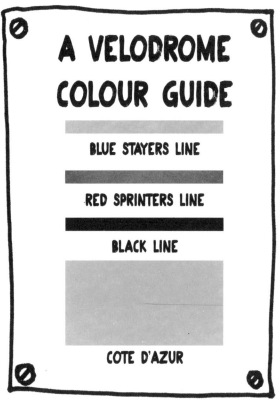

A VELODROME COLOUR GUIDE

BLUE STAYERS LINE

RED SPRINTERS LINE

BLACK LINE

COTE D'AZUR

THE STAGE IS DUE TO FINISH IN THIS OLD VELODROME AND BY THE LOOK OF IT SOMEONE HASN'T PAINTED IN THE LINES.

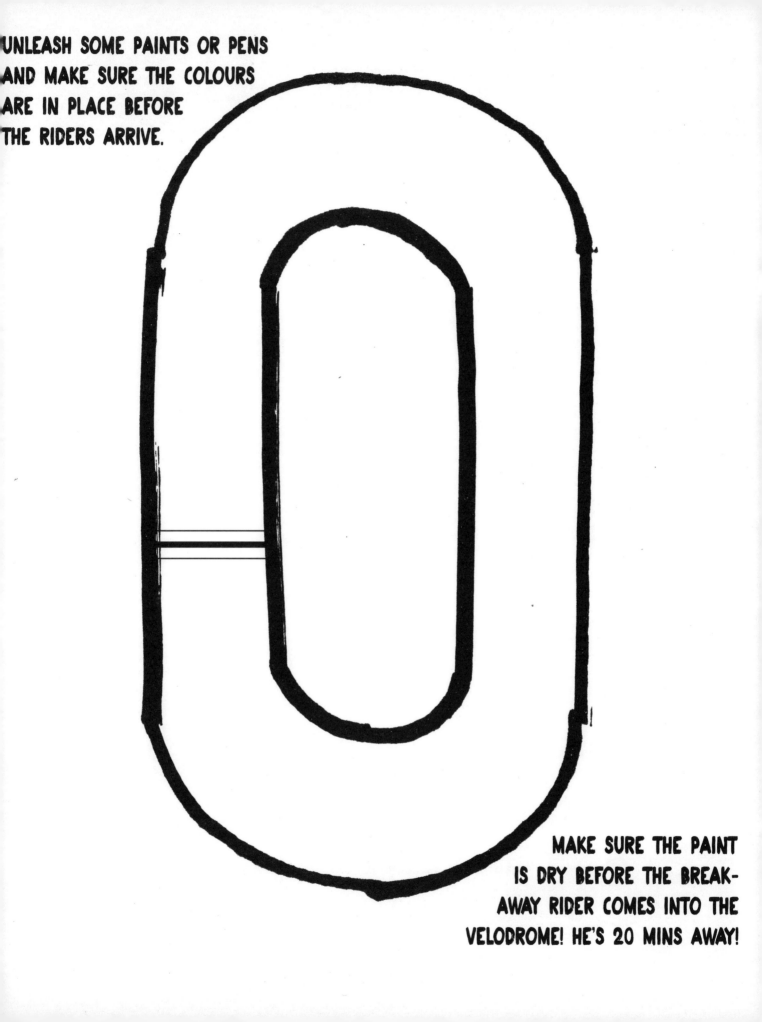

UNLEASH SOME PAINTS OR PENS AND MAKE SURE THE COLOURS ARE IN PLACE BEFORE THE RIDERS ARRIVE.

MAKE SURE THE PAINT IS DRY BEFORE THE BREAK-AWAY RIDER COMES INTO THE VELODROME! HE'S 20 MINS AWAY!

DESIGN THE JERSEY

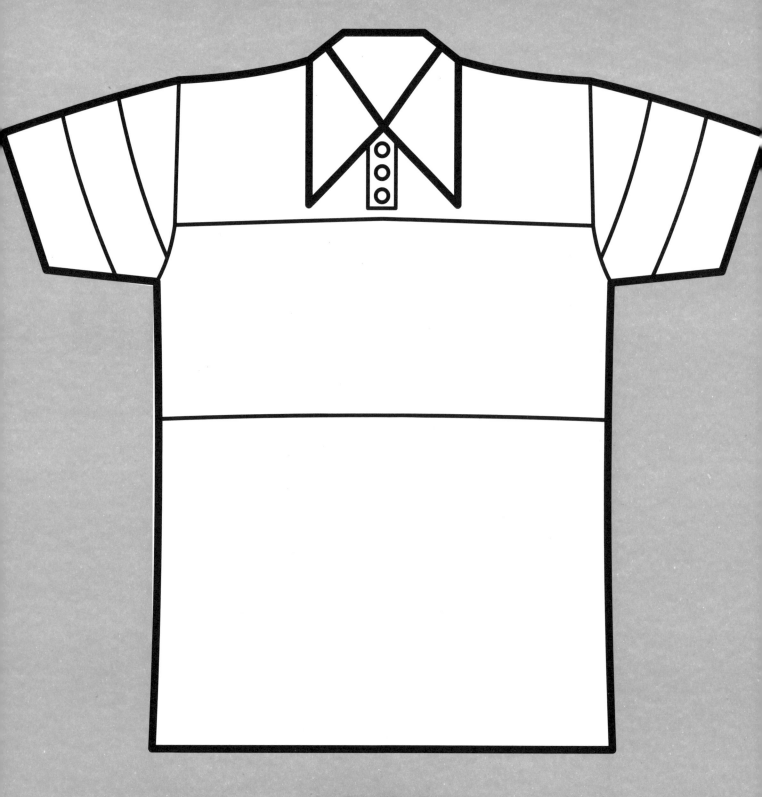

1950s

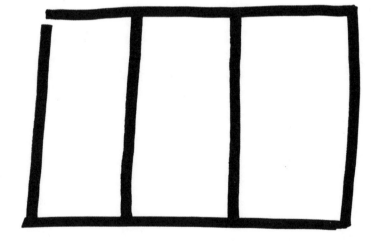

THE 1974 GIRO D'ITALIA

ROUTE BOOK

STAGE 9

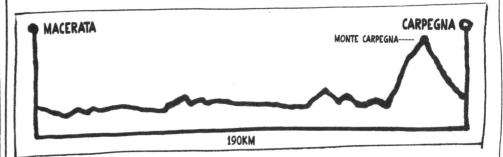

MACERATA

MONTE CARPEGNA-----

CARPEGNA

190KM

AN INCREDIBLY TOUGH STAGE IN THE 1974 GIRO FROM MACERATE, UP THE MONTE CARPEGNA AND DOWN THE TREACHEROUS DECENT TO THE FINISH AT CARPEGNA. A NERVOUS DAY, WITH CRASHES EARLY ON AND RIDERS FIGHTING FOR POSITION. THE LEADERS ARE MOVING FAST, TAKING THE OPPORTUNITY TO PUT THEIR RIVALS TO THE SWORD. AS THE RACE REACHES THE MONTE CARPEGNA, JOSE MANUAL FUENTE MAKES A BREAK FOR IT. HE SEES THIS AS HIS CHANCE TO TAKE TIME ON MERCKX. BUT MERCKX CHASES... FUENTE SUMMITS THE MONTE CARPEGNA FIRST, AND MERCKX COMES OVER SECOND. MIST AND RAIN COVER THE ROAD ON THE RUN IN TO THE FINISH BUT FUENTE SEES THIS AS HIS CHANCE TO TAKE THE MAGLIA ROSA OVERALL AND WINS THE STAGE, INCREASING HIS LEAD OVER MERCKX TO 1MIN 40SEC, BUT WILL THIS BE ENOUGH?

WHERE WERE YOU THAT DAY? HOW WERE YOUR LEGS FEELING AND DID YOUR TEAM DO ENOUGH TO PUT YOU IN THE RIGHT PLACE TO KEEP YOUR OVERALL POSITION SECURE ON GC?

WRITE YOUR ACCOUNT OF THE DAY ON THE NEXT PAGE, ADD IN LOTS OF DETAILS. HOW DID IT FEEL CHASING MERCKX AND FUENTE?

DRESS THE RIDER

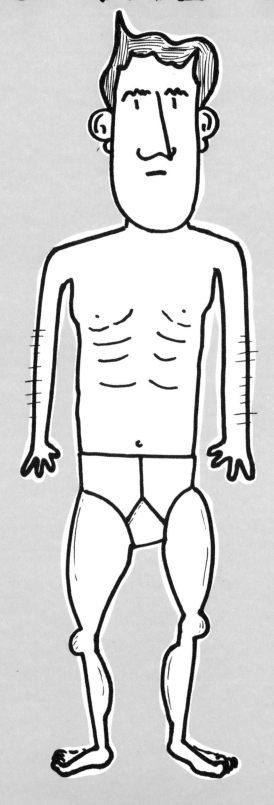

1950s

YOUR TOP TEN RIDERS...

1. _____

2. _____

3. _____

4. _____

5. _____

6. _____

7. _____

8. _____

9. _____

10. _____

THE TEAM MECHANIC HAS FITTED YOUR NUMBER.

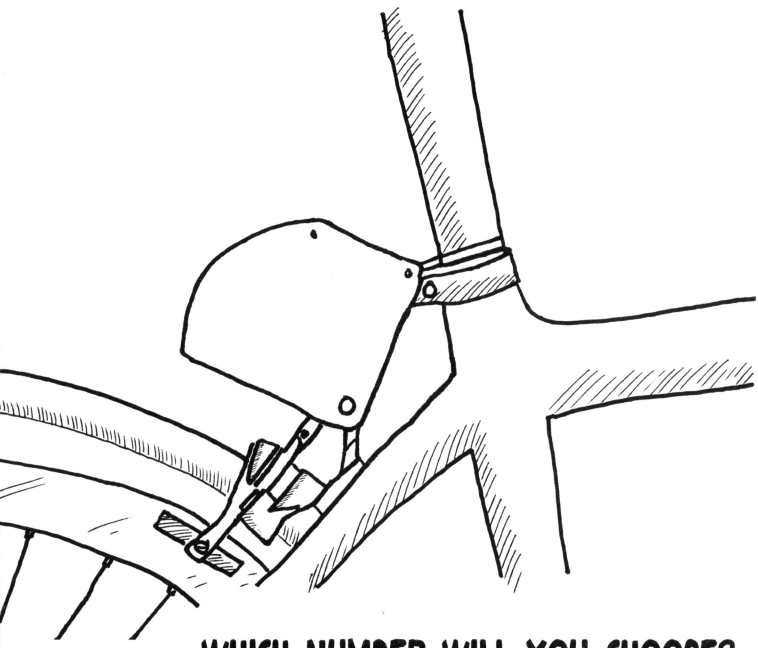

WHICH NUMBER WILL YOU CHOOSE?
FOR A TEAM IT MUST END IN A
NUMBER BETWEEN 1 AND 9.

YOUR TOP TEN TEAMS...

1. _____

2. _____

3. _____

4. _____

5. _____

6. _____

7. _____

8. _____

9. _____

10. _____

1	2	3	4	5	6	7	8	
11	12	13	14	15	16	17	18	
21	22	23	24	25	26	27	28	2
31	32	33	34	35	36	37	38	3
41	42	43	44	45	46	47	48	4
51	52	53	54	55	56	57	58	5
61	62	63	64	65	66	67	68	6
71	72	73	74	75	76	77	78	
81	92	83	84	85	86	87	88	8
91	92	93	94	95	96	97	98	9
101	102	103	104	105	106	107	108	10
111	112	113	114	115	116	117	118	11

YOUR TEAM HAVE BEEN CALLED TO SIGN ON

121	122	123	124	125	126	127	128	129
131	132	133	134	135	136	137	138	139
141	142	143	144	145	146	147	148	149
151	152	153	154	155	156	157	158	159
161	162	163	164	165	166	167	168	169
171	172	173	174	175	176	177	178	179
181	182	183	184	185	186	187	188	189
191	192	193	194	195	196	197	198	199
201	202	203	204	205	206	207	208	209
211	212	213	214	215	216	217	218	217

FIND YOUR CHOSEN NUMBER AND SIGN.

NINE SPOTS ON THE TEAM FOR THIS YEAR'S GIRO. WHO'S ON GOOD FORM? WHO'S PREPARED WELL IN THE MONTHS BEFOREHAND? EVERYONE WILL WANT THE CHANCE TO RIDE... WHICH NINE MAKE THE GRADE, AND WHO WILL BE THE BEST TEAM PLAYERS FOR YOUR LEADER?

RIDER NAME:_____

RIDER NAME:_____

RIDER NAME:_____

RIDER NAME:_____

RIDER NAME:_____

RIDER NAME:_____

RIDER NAME:_____

RIDER NAME:_____

COLOUR THE BIKES, MAKE
THEM BOLD. MAKE THEM
STAND OUT. MAY IN ITALY
IS OFTEN DAMP, SO MAKE
YOUR BIKES SHINE THROUGH
THE MIRK.

RIDER NAME:_____

THE TEAM BUS IS READY TO GO FOR ANOTHER GRAND TOUR! IT'S GOING TO BE COSY ABOARD 'OLD BETTY' FOR THREE WEEKS BUT THE TEAM ALL GET ON SO YOU'RE GOING TO HAVE A BLAST.

THE GLOBAL CYCLING NETWORK (GCN) CAME ROUND TO DO A TEAM BUS TOUR EARLIER! IT MIGHT HAVE BEEN THEIR SHORTEST VIDEO YET.

MAKE SURE TO COLOUR THE TEAM BUS IN YOUR TEAM COLOURS, AND ADD IN THE SPONSORS' LOGOS SO THE FANS KNOW WHERE TO FLOCK TO WHEN YOU AND THE TEAM TAKE THIS RACE BY THE SCRUFF OF THE NECK AND MAKE CYCLING HISTORY.

YOU'VE BEEN IN THE BREAK ALL DAY. THE SPRINTERS' TEAMS ARE GATHERING AT THE FRONT OF THE BUNCH. YOU'VE 10KM TO GO... WHAT TIME GAP DO YOU NEED TO WIN? HOW ARE THE LEGS FEELING? CAN YOU MAKE IT IN TIME?

MEANWHILE... ON THE STELVIO

OUR FAN IS FIRST HERE, BUT THIS IS THE STELVIO PASS AND HE KNEW THAT THE ONLY WAY TO SEE HIS HEROES WAS TO GET HERE AT LEAST A WEEK BEFORE. THE CAMPER VAN IS FURTHER DOWN THE ROAD. BUT SLOWLY THE ROAD IS FILLING UP! DRAW IN THE OTHER FANS, THE ROAD, AND THE NAMES ON THE ROAD, BE CREATIVE! FILL THE PAGES.

COPY COPPI

SOME OF FAUSTO COPPI'S MAJOR WINS:

GRAND TOURS

GIRO D'ITALIA
GENERAL CLASSIFICATION (1940, 1947, 1949, 1952, 1953)
MOUNTAIN CLASSIFICATION (1948, 1949, 1954)
22 INDIVIDUAL STAGES (1940-1955)

TOUR DE FRANCE
GENERAL CLASSIFICATION (1949, 1952)
MOUNTAIN CLASSIFICATION (1949, 1952)
9 INDIVIDUAL STAGES (1949-1952)

ONE-DAY RACES AND CLASSICS

MILAN-SAN REMO (1946, 1948, 1949)
PARIS-ROUBAIX (1950)
GIRO DI LOMBARDIA (1946, 1947, 1948, 1949, 1954)
LA FLÈCHE WALLONNE (1950)

DOT TO DOTTI

GRAND PRIX DES NATIONS (1946, 1947)
NATIONAL ROAD RACE CHAMPIONSHIPS (1942, 1945, 1949, 1955)
GIRO DELL'EMILIA (1941, 1947, 1948)
GIRO DELLA ROMAGNA (1946, 1947, 1949)

GIRO DEL VENETO (1941, 1947, 1949)
TRE VALLI VARESINE (1941, 1948, 1955)
HOUR RECORD (1942)

WORLD CHAMPIONSHIPS

GOLD MEDAL – 1953 – LUGANO
BRONZE MEDAL – 1949 – COPENHAGEN

DESIGN THE JERSEY

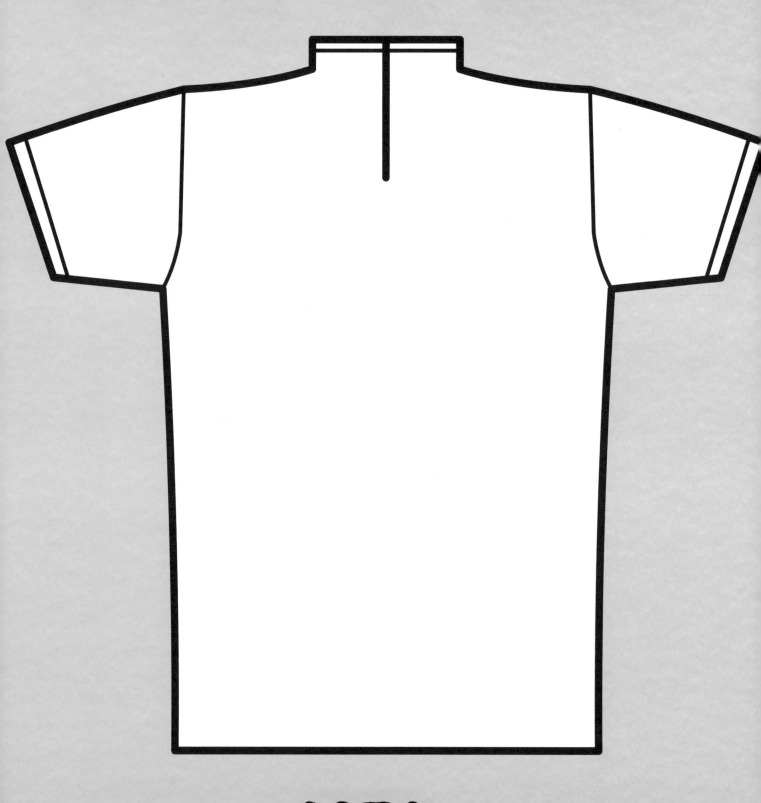

1970s

DRESS THE RIDER

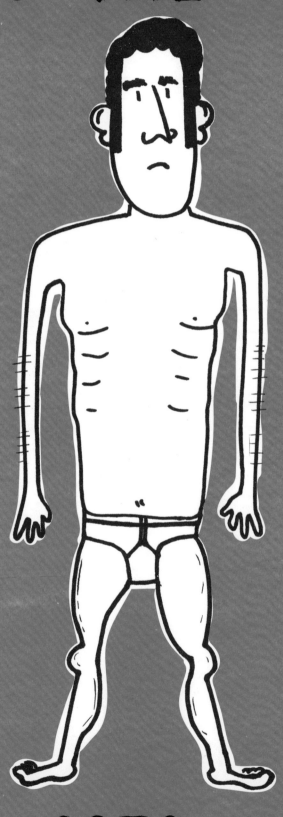

1970s

EDDY MERCKX LEGEND.

GET YOUR THINKING CAP ON.
DESIGN A NEW JERSEY.
THINK ABOUT THE TEAMS HE WAS PART OF:
SOLO SUPERIA, PEUGEOT-BP-MICHELIN,
FAEMA, MOLTENI

THE TEAM KNOW THAT YOUR TT POSITION COULD DO WITH SOME SERIOUS WORK AFTER THAT RACE LAST SEASON. SO YOU'VE BEEN FLOWN TO THE WIND TUNNEL AND AN AERODYNAMICS BOFFIN IS ABOUT TO GET TO WORK... DRAW YOUR PERFECT POSITION ON THE BIKE AND IF YOU WANT TO GET REALLY TECHNICAL, SHOW HOW THE AIR IS GOING TO FLOW OVER YOU LIKE A SLIPPERY EEL!

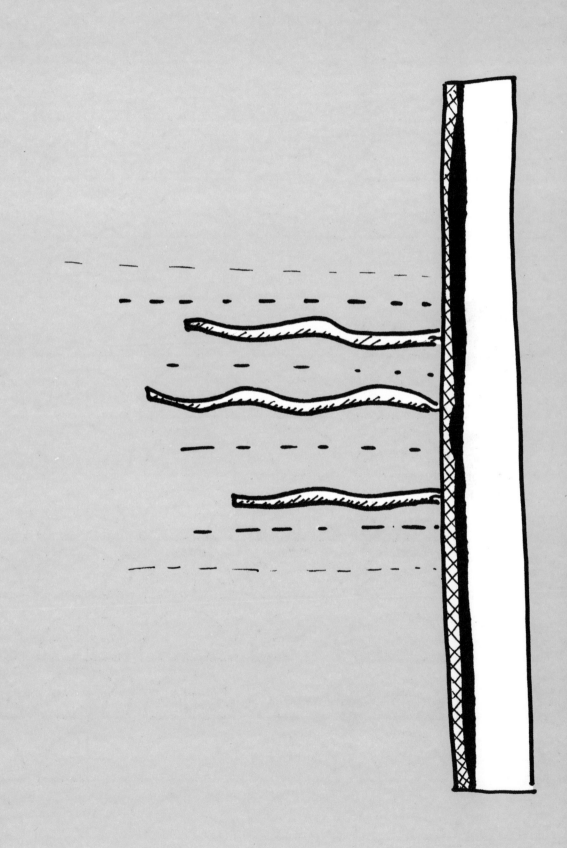

TOUR DE FRANCE

JULY. 21 STAGES. 3,500KM ISH.

THIS JULY FRANCE IS YOURS.
THE ROUTE IS UP TO YOU...

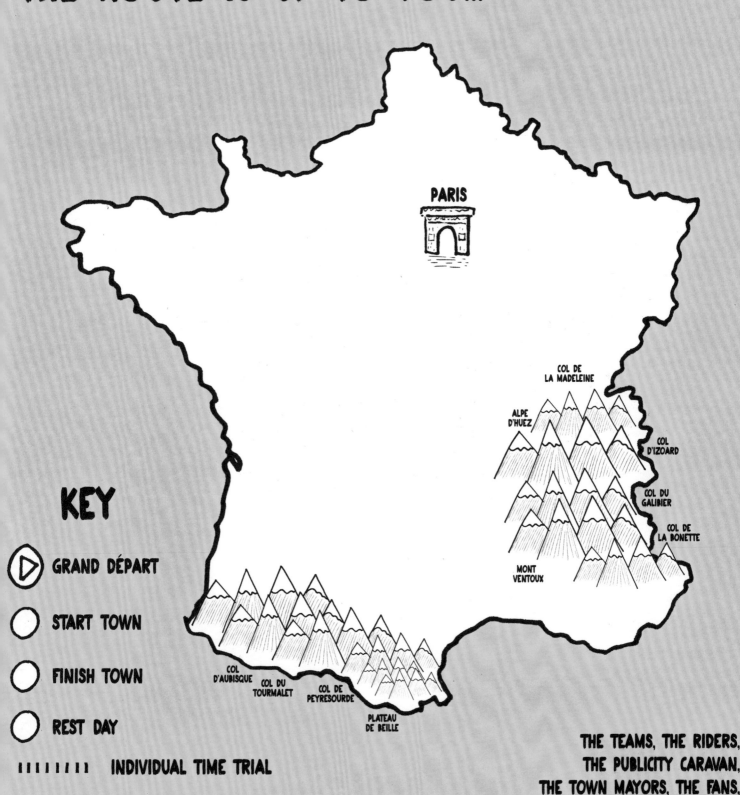

NINE SPOTS ON THE TEAM FOR THIS YEAR'S TOUR. IT'S NEARLY JULY AND THE EYES OF THE WORLD WILL BE ON CYCLING AND YOUR TEAM. WHOSE LIGHT IS BRIGHT? WHICH RIDER IN THE TEAM CAN WIN THE WORLD'S BIGGEST BIKE RACE? WHICH RIDERS ARE GOING TO SUPPORT THEM IN THAT QUEST FOR VICTORY?

RIDER NAME:_____   RIDER NAME:_____

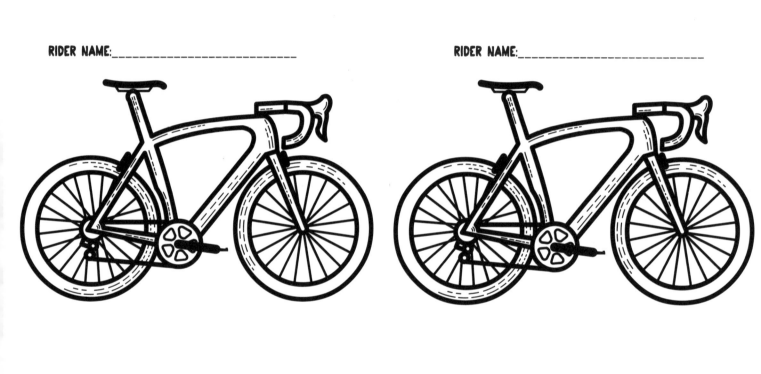

RIDER NAME:_____   RIDER NAME:_____

RIDER NAME:_____

RIDER NAME:_____

RIDER NAME:_____

RIDER NAME:_____

COLOUR THE BIKES, MAKE THEM BOLD. MAKE THEM STAND OUT. CREATE SOMETHING NEW FOR THE TEAM. THE WORLD IS WATCHING. THE SPONSORS ARE WATCHING!

RIDER NAME:_____

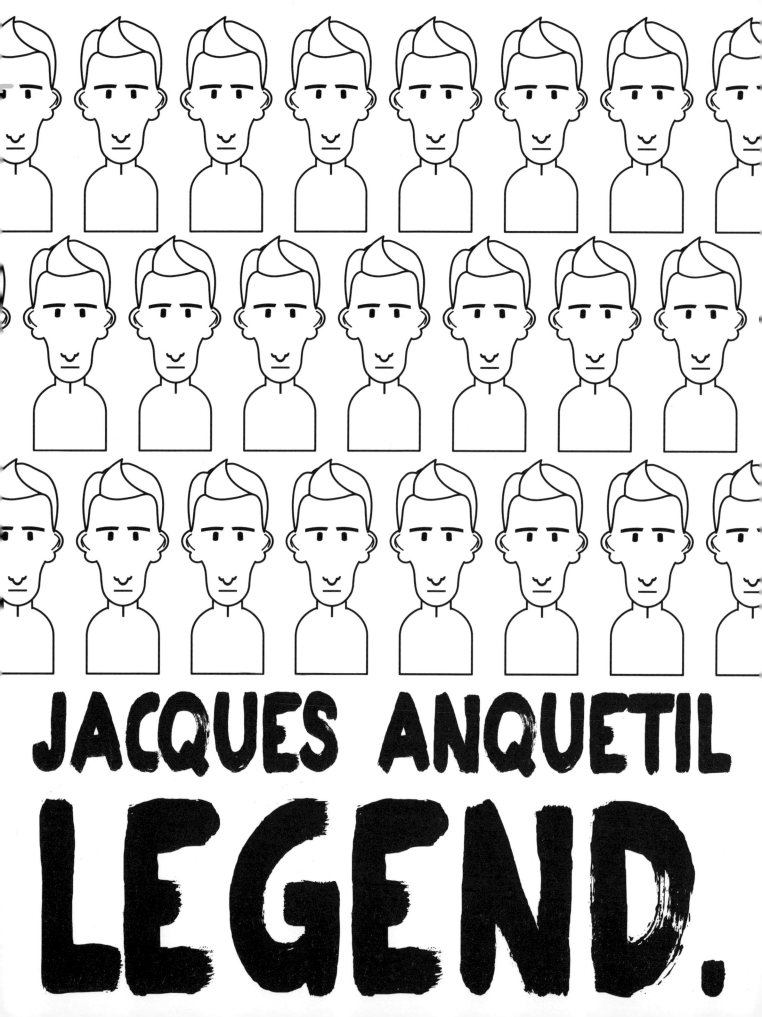

JACQUES ANQUETIL
LEGEND.

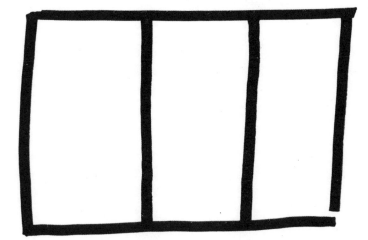

THE 1989 TOUR DE FRANCE

ROUTE BOOK

STAGE 19

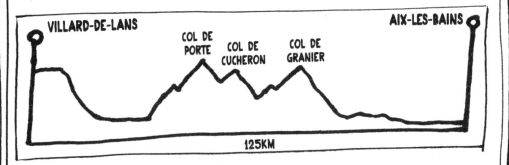

VILLARD-DE-LANS   COL DE   COL DE   COL DE   AIX-LES-BAINS
                                   PORTE   CUCHERON   GRANIER

125KM

FIGNON SITS IN YELLOW, 50 SECONDS AHEAD OF LEMOND ON GC. THIS STAGE TO
AIX-LES-BAINS (THE LAST MOUNTAIN STAGE OF THIS TOUR DE FRANCE) IS CRUCIAL.
ON THE COL DE PORTE A SMALL GROUP OF GC FAVOURITES HAVE GONE CLEAR,
STAMPING THEIR INTENT ON THE DAY. FIGNON AND LEMOND ARE THERE. ON THE
COL DE CUCHERON THEY ARE STILL TOGETHER AND, AS THEY APPROACH THE
SUMMIT OF THE COL DE GRANIER, LEMOND LAUNCHES HIS FINAL ATTACK BUT IS
BROUGHT BACK BY FIGNON WHO CAN'T PUT A FOOT WRONG THAT DAY. AS THEY
APPROACH THE FINISH AT AIX-LES-BAINES LEMOND SPRINTS FOR THE LINE, TAKING
THE WIN ON THE DAY AND KEEPING HIS GAP TO FIGNON AT 50 SECONDS. BUT
THERE ARE STILL TWO STAGES LEFT...

WHERE WERE YOU THAT DAY? HOW WERE YOUR LEGS FEELING AND DID YOUR TEAM
DO ENOUGH TO PUT YOU IN THE RIGHT PLACE TO KEEP YOUR OVERALL POSITION
SECURE ON GC?

WRITE YOUR ACCOUNT OF THE DAY ON THE NEXT PAGE, ADD IN LOTS OF DETAILS.
HOW DID IT FEEL CHASING FIGNON AND LEMOND IN SUCH A LEGENDARY TOUR?

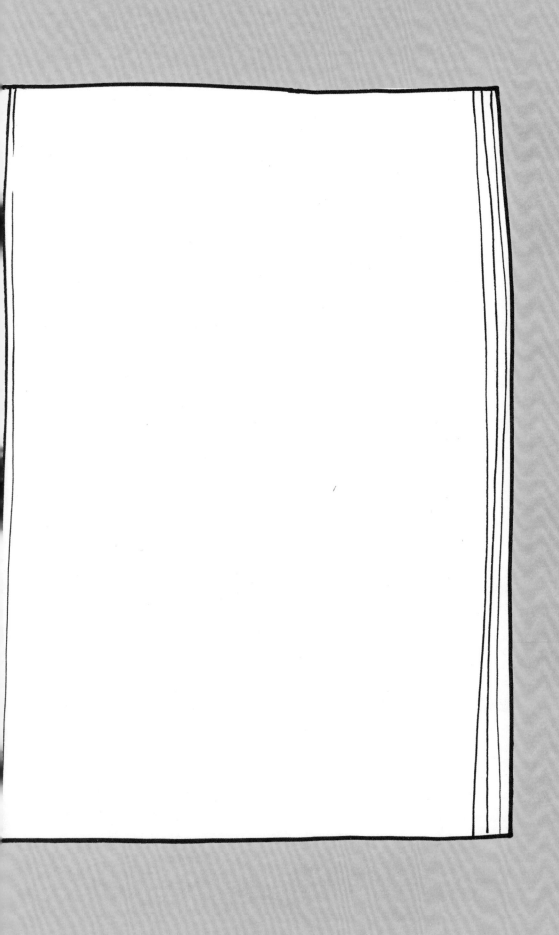

EACH CURRENT PRO CYCLING TEAM HAS IT'S OWN DISTINCT [ISH] COLOUR PALETTE... COLOUR EACH BOX IN JUST THAT COLOUR PALETTE. NO LOGOS, NO SPONSORS' NAMES, JUST COLOUR. THINKING CAP ON, CAN YOU RE-CREATE THEM ALL FROM MEMORY?

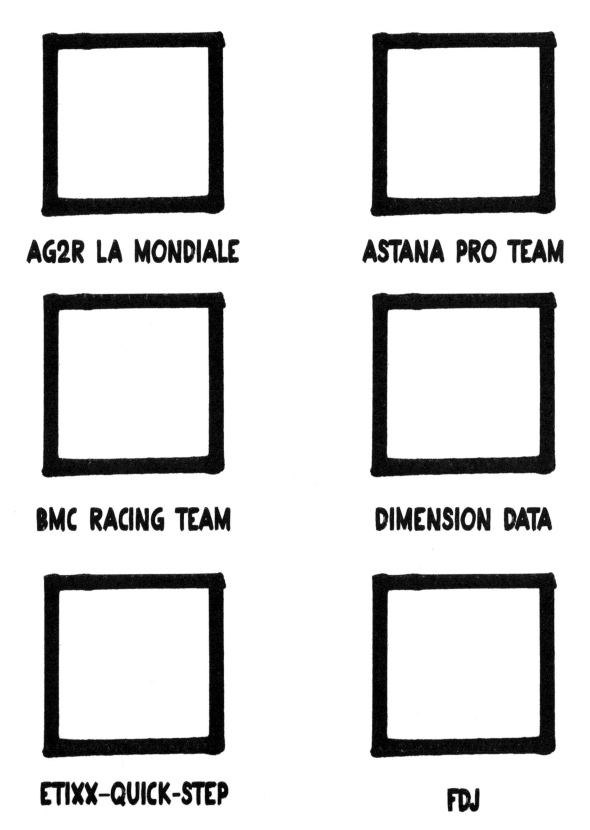

AG2R LA MONDIALE

ASTANA PRO TEAM

BMC RACING TEAM

DIMENSION DATA

ETIXX-QUICK-STEP

FDJ

IAM CYCLING

LAMPRE MERIDA

LOTTO SOUDAL

MOVISTAR TEAM

ORICA GREENEDGE

CANNONDALE PRO CYCLING TEAM

DRESS THE RIDER

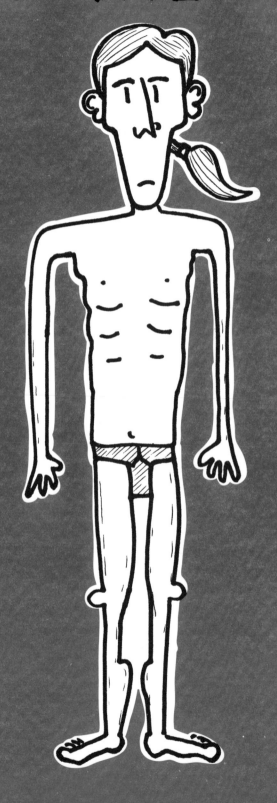

1980s

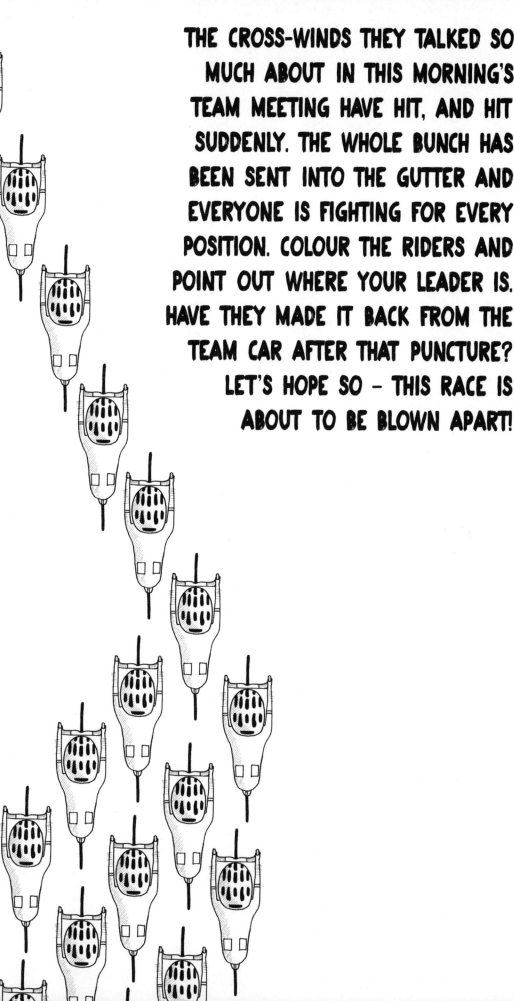

THE CROSS-WINDS THEY TALKED SO MUCH ABOUT IN THIS MORNING'S TEAM MEETING HAVE HIT, AND HIT SUDDENLY. THE WHOLE BUNCH HAS BEEN SENT INTO THE GUTTER AND EVERYONE IS FIGHTING FOR EVERY POSITION. COLOUR THE RIDERS AND POINT OUT WHERE YOUR LEADER IS. HAVE THEY MADE IT BACK FROM THE TEAM CAR AFTER THAT PUNCTURE? LET'S HOPE SO – THIS RACE IS ABOUT TO BE BLOWN APART!

CUT OUT AND KEEP YOUR OWN

CAMPING BY THE SIDE OF THE ROAD FOR THE LAST THREE WEEKS TO KEEP HIS SPOT, OUR SUPER FAN HAS BEEN LIVING ON A DIET OF BBQ, BEER AND 90s' EURO TRANCE... EVERY YEAR HE MAKES THE PILGRIMAGE TO THE SAME MOUNTAIN TO EAT, SLEEP AND DRINK THIS GRAND TOUR. HE CONSIDERS IT A VICTORY TO GET ON THE TV COVERAGE, SO MAKE HIM STAND OUT IN THE CROWD! CUT OUT, COLOUR AND DRESS HIM! QUICK! THOSE PANTS ARE GROSS!

CYCLING MEGA FAN!!!

(WHO MIGHT BE A BIT DRUNK)

THE BIG HORNED HELMET. THERE'S NOT MANY BIGGER HORNS IN CYCLING THAN THIS

USA

ROUND SUNGLASSES

80s' OAKLEY RETRO SUNGLASSES

STAR SHAPED GLASSES! BECAUSE WE'RE ALL DIVAS ONCE IN A WHILE

A WATCH. CAUSE IT'S NICE TO KNOW THE TIME...

THE TV CAMERAS LOVE SOMEONE RUNNING NEXT TO THE RIDERS IN A SNORKEL - HONEST!

CLOWN PANTS!

GET SNIPPING!

SMOKING IS NOT COOL... UNLESS YOU'RE DRUNK WATCHING BIKE RACING.

BRRRRR IT'S FRESH OUT! BEST POP THIS BOBBLE HAT ON!

VERY STRONG BEER

VERY STRONG BEER

VERY STRONG BEER

CYCLING ROCKS

CYCLING DOES ROCK! I THINK EVERY SUPER FAN NEEDS THIS SHIRT

VERY STRONG BEER

VERY STRONG BEER

VERY STRONG BEER

IF THERE'S SNOW ON THE STELVIO THESE FUR LINED ELF BOOTS LOOK DAFT BUT WILL KEEP YOU WARM!

IT WOULDN'T BE A BIKE RACE UNLESS THERE WAS VERY STRONG EURO BEER! FILL YOUR BOOTS SUPER FAN!

MANKINI!!!!!!!!

SNEAK ANOTHER... NO ONE'S WATCHING...

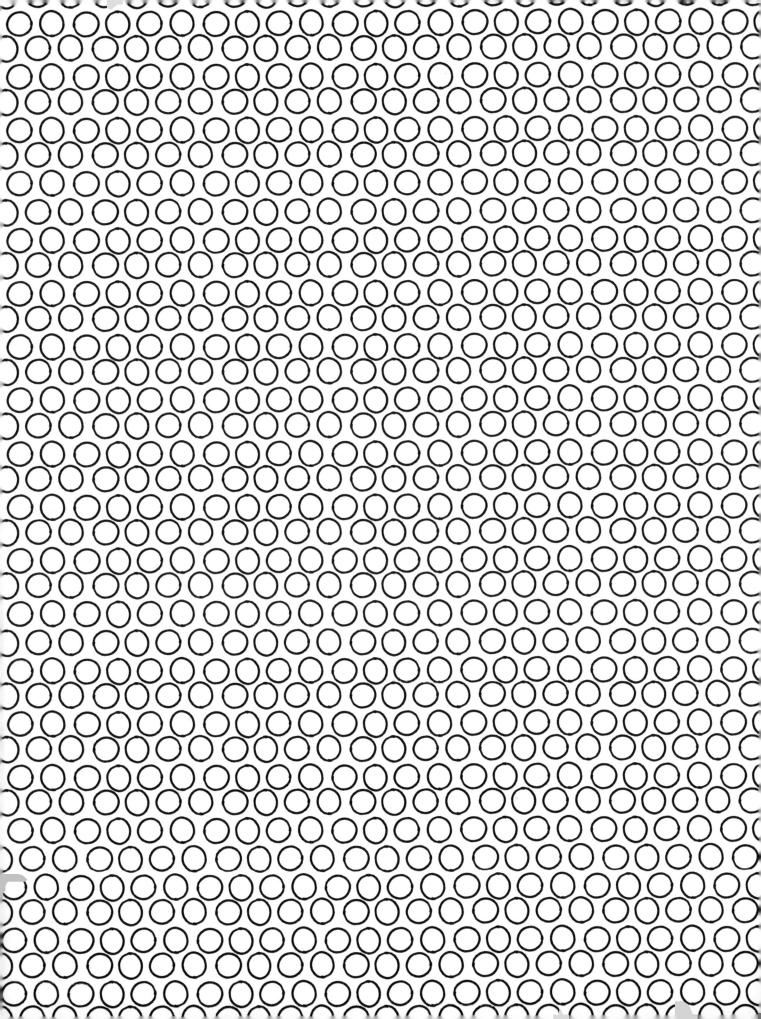

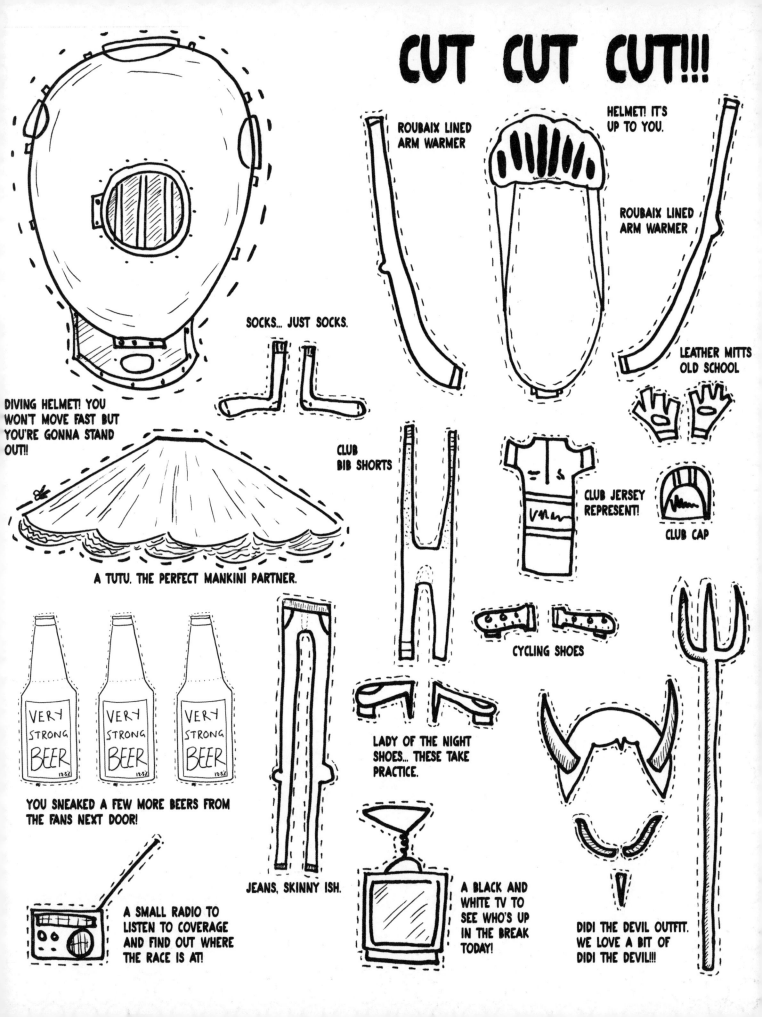

CUT CUT CUT!!!

ROUBAIX LINED ARM WARMER

HELMET! IT'S UP TO YOU.

ROUBAIX LINED ARM WARMER

LEATHER MITTS OLD SCHOOL

SOCKS... JUST SOCKS.

DIVING HELMET! YOU WON'T MOVE FAST BUT YOU'RE GONNA STAND OUT!!

CLUB BIB SHORTS

CLUB JERSEY REPRESENT!

CLUB CAP

A TUTU. THE PERFECT MANKINI PARTNER.

VERY STRONG BEER

VERY STRONG BEER

VERY STRONG BEER

CYCLING SHOES

LADY OF THE NIGHT SHOES... THESE TAKE PRACTICE.

YOU SNEAKED A FEW MORE BEERS FROM THE FANS NEXT DOOR!

JEANS, SKINNY ISH.

A SMALL RADIO TO LISTEN TO COVERAGE AND FIND OUT WHERE THE RACE IS AT!

A BLACK AND WHITE TV TO SEE WHO'S UP IN THE BREAK TODAY!

DIDI THE DEVIL OUTFIT. WE LOVE A BIT OF DIDI THE DEVIL!!!

YOUR TOP TEN MOUNTAINS...

1. _____

2. _____

3. _____

4. _____

5. _____

6. _____

7. _____

8. _____

9. _____

10. _____

REMEMBER THAT TEAM? AND THAT ONE? AND THE JERSEY THEY RACED IN? NOW'S YOUR CHANCE TO SHOW SOME REAL KNOWLEDGE OF CYCLING'S PAST BY COLOURING IN THE SQUARES IN THE COLOURS OF SOME OF THE MOST FAMOUS TEAMS FROM CYCLING'S PAST. TRY TO DO THIS FROM MEMORY!

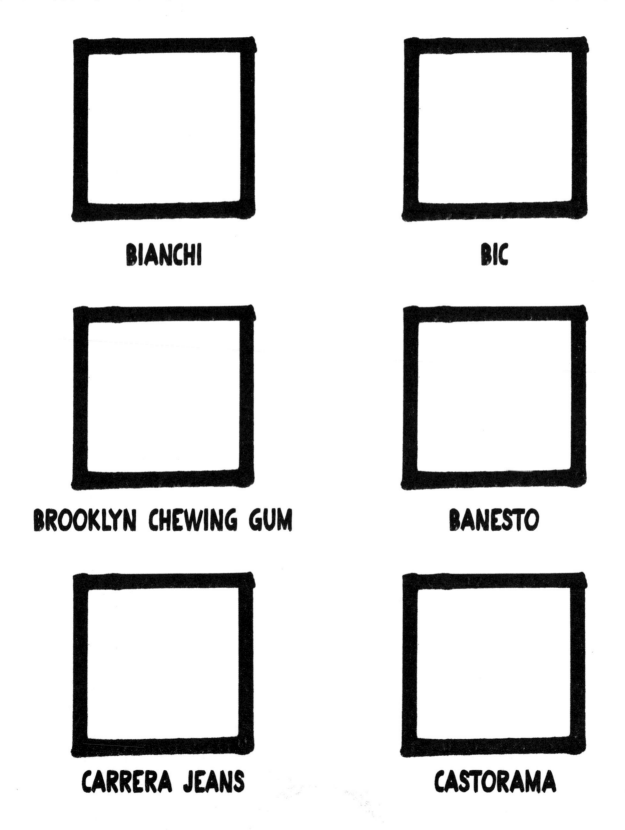

BIANCHI

BIC

BROOKLYN CHEWING GUM

BANESTO

CARRERA JEANS

CASTORAMA

DEL TONGO COLNAGO

EUSKALTEL EUSKADI

MAPEI

MOTOROLA

ONCE

RENAULT ELF

MONSIEUR CHRONO

SOME OF JACQUES ANQUETIL'S MAJOR WINS:

GRAND TOURS

GIRO D'ITALIA
GENERAL CLASSIFICATION (1960, 1964)
5 INDIVIDUAL STAGES

TOUR DE FRANCE
GENERAL CLASSIFICATION (1957, 1961, 1962, 1963, 1964)
16 INDIVIDUAL STAGES

VUELTA A ESPAÑA
GENERAL CLASSIFICATION (1963)
1 INDIVIDUAL STAGE

THE DOT TO DOT

STAGE RACES

PARIS–NICE (1957, 1961, 1963, 1965, 1966)
FOUR DAYS OF DUNKIRK (1958, 1959)
CRITÉRIUM DU DAUPHINÉ LIBÉRÉ (1963, 1965)

ONE-DAY RACES AND CLASSICS

GENT–WEVELGEM (1964)
BORDEAUX–PARIS (1965)
LIÈGE–BASTOGNE–LIÈGE (1966)

HOUR RECORD (1956)
SUPER PRESTIGE PERNOD INTERNATIONAL (1961, 1963, 1965, 1966)
GRAND PRIX DES NATIONS (1953, 1954, 1955, 1956, 1957, 1958, 1961, 1965, 1966)

WORLD CHAMPIONSHIPS

SILVER – 1966 – NÜRBURGRING

MIGUEL INDURAIN
LEGEND.

GET YOUR THINKING CAP ON AND DESIGN BIG MIG A NEW JERSEY. THINK ABOUT THE TEAMS HE WAS PART OF: REYNOLDS, AND BANESTO.

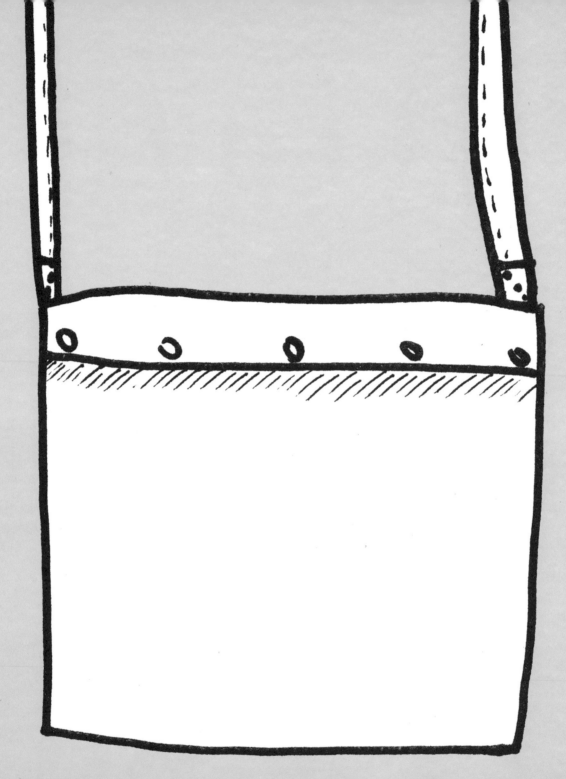

THIS IS THE TEAM MUSETTE — SLAP THE TEAM LOGOS ALL OVER IT. BE BOLD! YOU NEED IT TO STAND OUT SO YOU CAN GRAB IT EASILY IN THE CHAOS OF THE FEEDZONE.

BANANA

WRAPPED RICE CAKES

BOTTLE OF WATER

BOTTLE OF ENERGY MIX

ENERGY GEL WITH CAFFEINE [FOR THE FINAL PUSH]

SMALL CAKE

HAM AND CHEESE SANDWICH

A CAN OF SWEET FIZZY BROWN

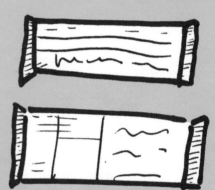

ENERGY BARS X2

THE SOIGNEURS ARE PACKING YOUR MUSETTE FOR THE NEXT STAGE. COLOUR IN ALL THE STUFF YOU WANT IN THE BAG... LOOKING AT THE STAGE PROFILE FOR TOMORROW I'D GO WITH IT ALL. IT'S GOING TO BE TOUGH.

THE ROAD ON THIS STAGE SNAKES ACROSS A VAST MOUNTAIN RANGE... DRAW THAT ROAD. HOW MANY TIMES WILL YOU TAKE THE RIDERS UP THE MOUNTAINS? IT'S UP TO YOU!

ONE LAST CLIMB. THIS IS THE MOUNTAIN YOU CAME TO TAKE A LOOK AT DURING THE SPRING. THERE'S BEEN A PICTURE OF IT ON YOUR WALL SINCE YOU WERE A KID. YOU'RE ALONE OUT FRONT. THIS IS YOUR MOMENT. WITH 20KMS TO GO THE MOTO PULLS UP TO YOU AND LETS YOU KNOW HOW FAR THE MAIN CON-TENDERS ARE BEHIND YOU. FILL IN THE TIME GAP. THERE'S BEEN THREE OTHER MOUNTAINS BEFORE THIS ONE. HOW MUCH HAVE YOU GOT LEFT?

MEANWHILE... AT DUTCH CORNER... ALPE D'HUEZ

OUR FAN IS FIRST HERE. HE CYCLED ALL THE WAY FROM
EINDHOVEN AND HAS PITCHED HIS CAMP A WHOLE MONTH BEFORE
THE RACE ARRIVES TO GET A GOOD SPOT. TIME FOR YOU TO
DRAW THE OTHER FANS AS THEY ARRIVE ON THIS MOST ICONIC
CORNER OF ALPE D'HUEZ. FILL THE PAGES. IT'S PACKED!

THE FANS HAVE GATHERED OUTSIDE THE TEAM BUS TO CATCH A GLIMPSE OF YOU AFTER THAT FANTASTIC RIDE! THIS YEAR'S RIDER CARDS NEVER APPEARED AFTER THE ITALIAN NOVELTY SHAPED LUNCHEON MEAT MANUFACTURER SPONSORING YOUR TEAM WENT BUST LAST MONTH... SO – IT'S UP TO YOU! DRAW YOURSELF IN TEAM KIT ON THE CARD, AND SIGN A FEW FOR THE WAITING FANS. THEY'VE BEEN THERE FOR HOURS. YOU'RE A HERO.

WRAP THE TEAM CAR IN YOUR SPONSORS'
LOGOS... BE CREATIVE. DON'T LET YOUR
CAR BE LOST IN THE CONVOY.

THE DIRECTEUR SPORTIF PULLS ALONGSIDE YOU IN THE BREAK... WHAT WORDS OF WISDOM IS HE SHOUTING THIS TIME???

DRESS THE RIDER

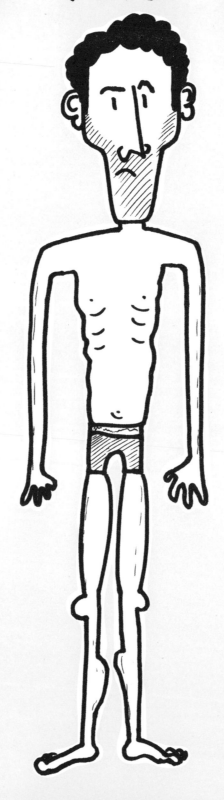

1990s

IT'S FINALLY HERE. DINNER TIME. EVERY PART OF YOU ACHES AFTER THAT STAGE. I'M NOT SURE YOU CAN EVEN MUSTER THE ENERGY TO LIFT YOUR FORK. BUT TOMORROW IS ANOTHER DAY. FILL YOUR BOOTS. PILE THAT PLATE HIGH.

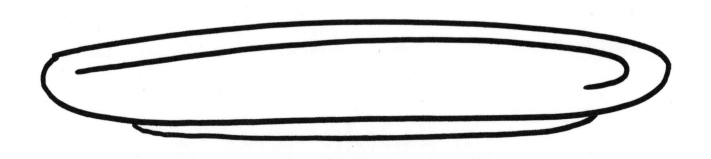

SIR BRADLEY WIGGINS
LEGEND.

GET YOUR THINKING CAP ON AND DESIGN SIR BRADLEY A NEW JERSEY. THINK ABOUT THE TEAMS HE HAS BEEN PART OF: THE LINDA MCCARTNEY RACING TEAM, FRANÇAISE DES JEUX, CRÉDIT AGRICOLE, COFIDIS, TEAM HIGH ROAD, GARMIN-SLIPSTREAM, TEAM SKY, TEAM WIGGINS, TEAM GB.

WE'RE INTO THE LAST 5KMS OF TODAY'S STAGE AND THE BREAK HAS BEEN CAUGHT. ALL THE SPRINTERS TEAMS HAVE GOT TO THE FRONT AND ARE DRIVING THINGS ALONG AT 60KM PER HOUR TO MAKE SURE NO ONE ELSE ESCAPES...

YOUR SPRINTER IS WEARING THE GREEN
JERSEY, FIND THEM IN THE BUNCH,
COLOUR THEM IN, AND MAKE SURE THEY
HAVE THEIR TEAM AND SPRINT TRAIN
READY FOR ACTION! GO GO GO GO!!!

LE BLAIREAU

SOME OF BERNARD HINAULT'S MAJOR WINS:

GRAND TOURS

GIRO D'ITALIA
GENERAL CLASSIFICATION (1980, 1982, 1985)
6 INDIVIDUAL STAGES (1980, 1982, 1985)

TOUR DE FRANCE
GENERAL CLASSIFICATION (1978, 1979, 1981, 1982, 1985)
POINTS CLASSIFICATION (1979)
MOUNTAIN CLASSIFICATION (1986)
COMBATIVITY AWARD (1981, 1984, 1986)
COMBINATION CLASSIFICATION (1981, 1982)
28 INDIVIDUAL STAGES (1978–1986)

VUELTA A ESPAÑA
GENERAL CLASSIFICATION (1978, 1983)
7 INDIVIDUAL STAGES (1978, 1983)

STAGE RACES
CRITÉRIUM DU DAUPHINÉ LIBÉRÉ (1977, 1979, 1981)
TOUR DE ROMANDIE (1980)

DOT TO DOT

ONE-DAY RACES AND CLASSICS
WORLD ROAD RACE CHAMPIONSHIPS (1980)
NATIONAL ROAD RACE CHAMPIONSHIPS (1978)
LIÈGE–BASTOGNE–LIÈGE (1977, 1980)
GIRO DI LOMBARDIA (1979, 1984)

PARIS–ROUBAIX (1981)
LA FLÈCHE WALLONNE (1979, 1983)
GHENT–WEVELGEM (1977)
AMSTEL GOLD RACE (1981)
GRAND PRIX DES NATIONS (1977,
1978, 1979, 1982, 1984)

WORLD CHAMPIONSHIPS

GOLD MEDAL – 1980 – SALANCHES
BRONZE MEDAL – 1981 – PRAGUE

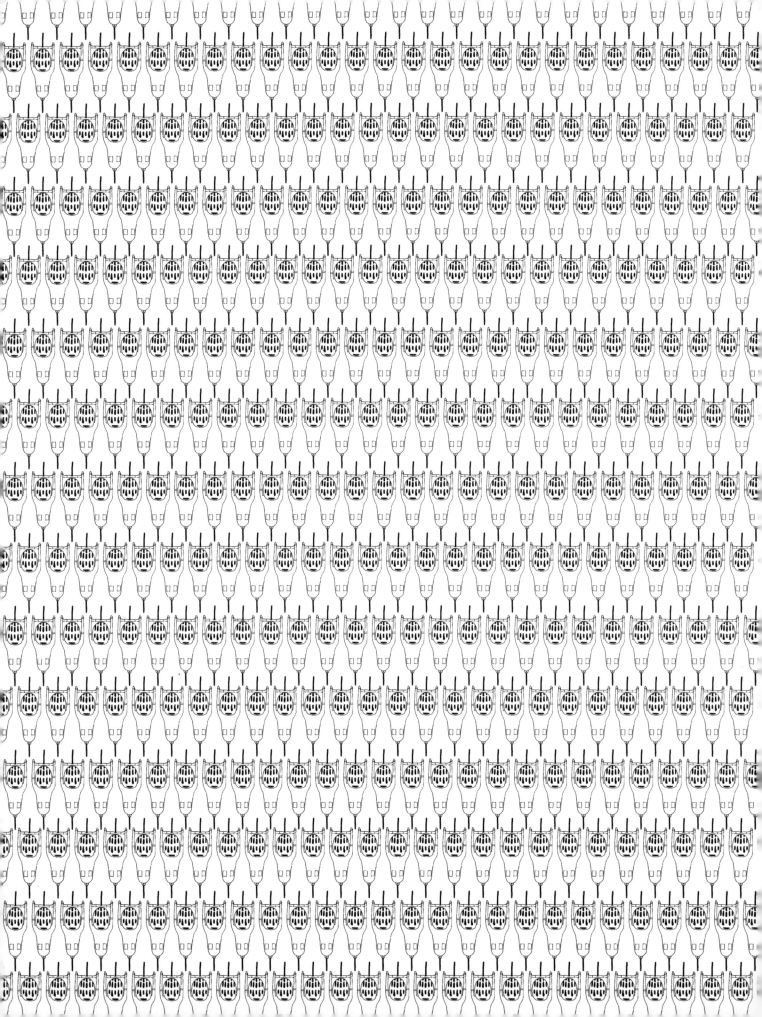

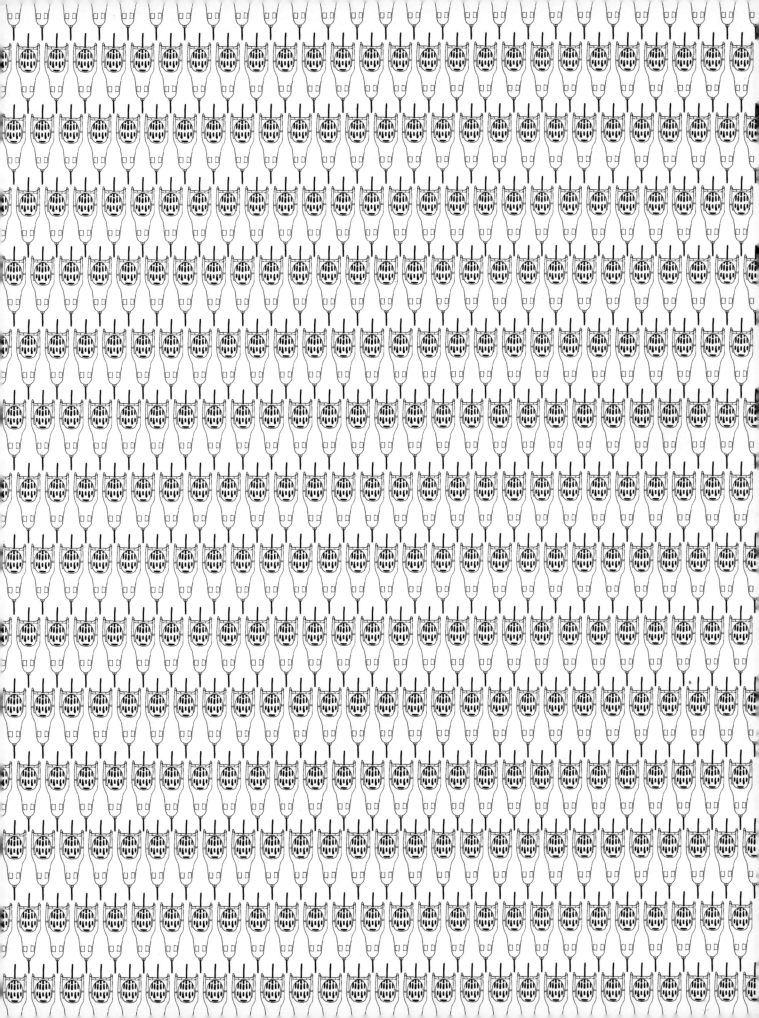

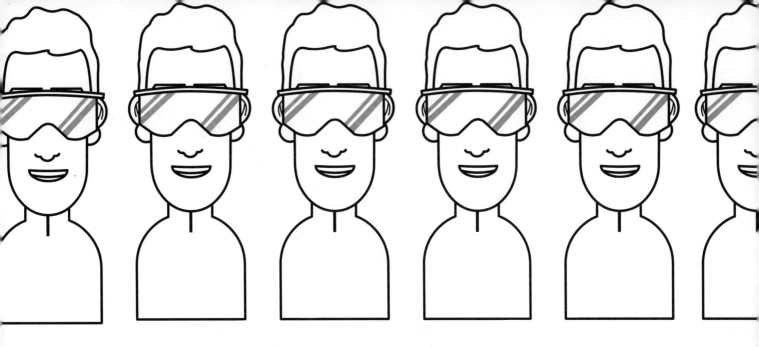

GREG LEMOND LEGEND.

GET YOUR THINKING CAP ON AND DESIGN GREG A NEW JERSEY. THINK ABOUT THE TEAMS HE WAS PART OF: RENAULT-ELF-GITANE, LA VIE CLAIRE, PDM, ADR, AND Z.

YOU DID IT! WHAT A RACE! THE PODIUM AWAITS. YOU'VE PERFORMED FAR BETTER THAN EVEN THE TEAM THOUGHT YOU COULD AND THIS RIDE COULD BE THE MAKING OF YOUR CAREER... DRAW WHICH STEP OF THE PODIUM YOU REACHED, AND WHICH RIDERS STAND AROUND YOU AT THIS FANTASTIC MOMENT!

COLOUR IN THE CHAMPS-ÉLYSÉES!

THE SUN IS SHINING, THE TREES SMELL SWEET IN THE AFTERNOON PARIS AIR. TAKE IT ALL IN. YOU'VE DREAMT OF THIS SINCE YOU WERE A CHILD.

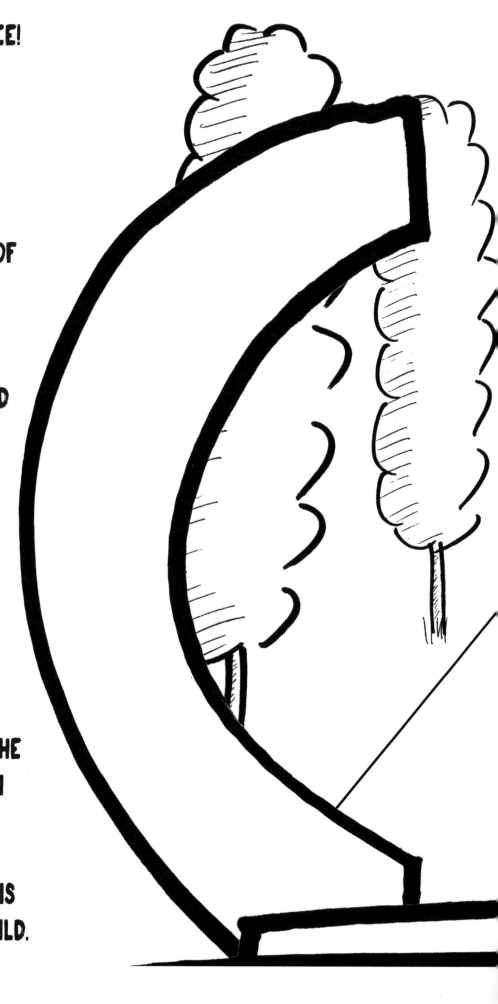

IT'S 06:30 ON A SATURDAY AND THERE'S A LARGE BANG ON YOUR DOOR... IT'S DOPING CONTROL. YOU OPEN THE DOOR, AND WITH A TIRED WELCOME, POP THE KETTLE ON. YOU THEN PROVIDE BOTH SAMPLES.

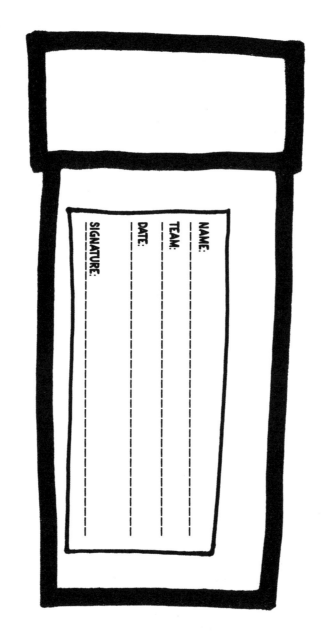

NAME:

TEAM:

DATE:

SIGNATURE:

A SAMPLE

COLOUR IN YOUR MORNING FLOW AND FILL IN ALL THE REQUIRED INFORMATION...

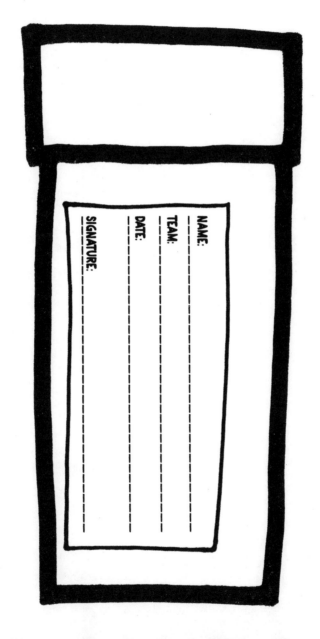

B SAMPLE

EACH CURRENT PRO CYCLING TEAM HAS IT'S OWN DISTINCT [ISH] COLOUR PALETTE... COLOUR EACH BOX IN JUST THAT COLOUR PALETTE! NO LOGOS, NO SPONSORS' NAMES, JUST COLOUR! THINKING CAP ON! CAN YOU RE-CREATE THEM ALL FROM MEMORY!

TEAM GIANT ALPECIN

TEAM KATUSHA

TEAM LOTTONL JUMBO

TEAM SKY

TINKOFF

TREK FACTORY RACING

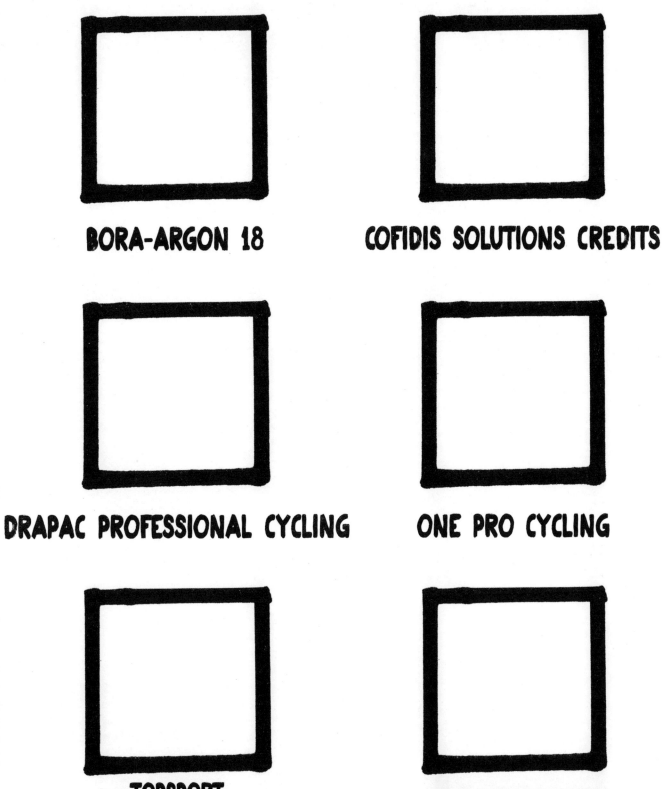

BORA-ARGON 18

COFIDIS SOLUTIONS CREDITS

DRAPAC PROFESSIONAL CYCLING

ONE PRO CYCLING

**TOPSPORT
VLAANDEREN-BALOISE**

**UNITEDHEALTHCARE
PROFESSIONAL CYCLING TEAM**

THE CANNIBAL

SOME OF EDDY MERCKX'S MAJOR WINS:

GIRO D'ITALIA
GENERAL CLASSIFICATION (1968, 1970, 1972, 1973, 1974)
POINTS CLASSIFICATION (1968, 1973)
MOUNTAINS CLASSIFICATION (1968)
24 INDIVIDUAL STAGES (1968–1974)

TOUR DE FRANCE
GENERAL CLASSIFICATION (1969, 1970, 1971, 1972, 1974)
POINTS CLASSIFICATION (1969, 1971, 1972)
MOUNTAINS CLASSIFICATION (1969, 1970)
COMBATIVITY AWARD (1969, 1970, 1974, 1975)
COMBINATION CLASSIFICATION (1969, 1970, 1971, 1972, 1974)
34 INDIVIDUAL STAGES (1969–1975)

VUELTA A ESPAÑA
GENERAL CLASSIFICATION (1973)
POINTS CLASSIFICATION (1973)
COMBINATION CLASSIFICATION (1973)
6 INDIVIDUAL STAGES (1973)

DOT TO DOT

STAGE RACES

PARIS–NICE: (1969, 1970, 1971)
TOUR DE SUISSE: (1974)

ONE-DAY RACES AND CLASSICS

MILAN–SAN REMO (1966, 1967, 1969, 1971,
1972, 1975, 1976)
TOUR OF FLANDERS (1969, 1975)
PARIS–ROUBAIX (1968, 1970, 1973)

LIÈGE–BASTOGNE–LIÈGE (1969, 1971, 1972,
1973, 1975)
GIRO DI LOMBARDIA (1971, 1972)
SUPER PRESTIGE PERNOD INTERNATIONAL (1969, 1970,
1971, 1972, 1973,
1974, 1975)
NATIONAL ROAD RACE CHAMPIONSHIPS (1970)
HOUR RECORD (1972)

WORLD CHAMPIONSHIPS

GOLD MEDAL – 1964 – SALLANCHES [AMATEUR]
GOLD MEDAL – 1967 – HEERLEN
GOLD MEDAL – 1971 – MENDRISIOF
GOLD MEDAL – 1974 – MONTRÉAL

VUELTA A ESPAÑA

SEPT. 21 STAGES. 3,500KM ISH.

I'M NOT SURE WHO HIRES THE ROUTE PEOPLE... THEY'VE FORGOTTEN THIS, AGAIN! BREAK OUT THE PENS, 21 STAGES. GO!

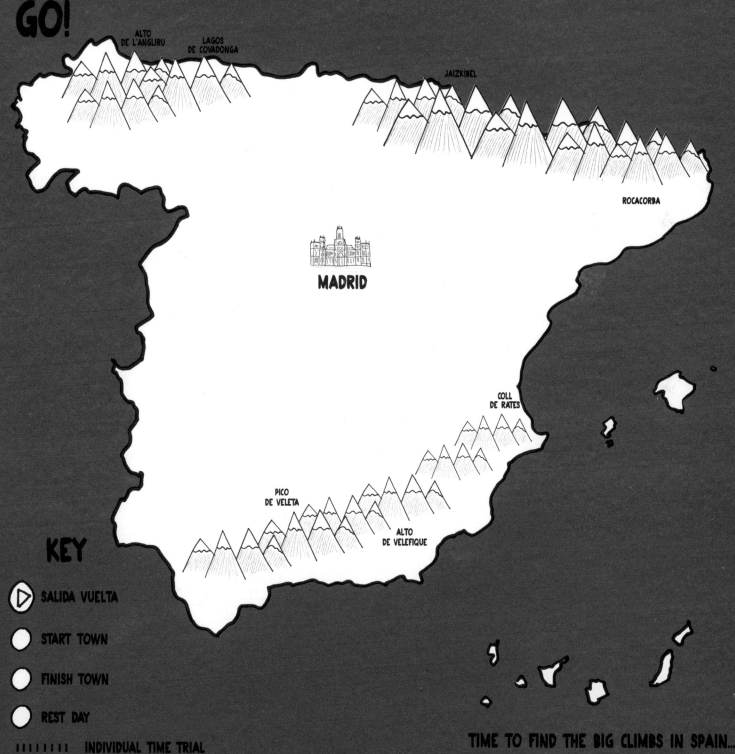

ALTO DE L'ANGLIRU

LAGOS DE COVADONGA

JAIZKIBEL

ROCACORBA

MADRID

COLL DE RATES

PICO DE VELETA

ALTO DE VELEFIQUE

KEY

▷ SALIDA VUELTA

◯ START TOWN

◯ FINISH TOWN

◯ REST DAY

|||||||| INDIVIDUAL TIME TRIAL

▪▪▪▪▪ TEAM TIME TRIAL

TIME TO FIND THE BIG CLIMBS IN SPAIN...
ADD THEM IN, ONE AFTER THE OTHER.
BRING THE PAIN!

NINE SPOTS ON THE TEAM FOR THIS YEAR'S VUELTA. IT'S BEEN A LONG SEASON FOR SOME OF YOUR TEAM. THEY RACED AND WON AS FAR BACK AS JANUARY AT THE TOUR DOWN UNDER BUT THEY'RE A GANG OF MATES. THEY CAN WIN THIS RACE AND TAKE HOME AT LEAST ONE JERSEY. MAKE YOUR PICK, AND GET THE BEER ON ICE FOR MADRID!

RIDER NAME:_____

RIDER NAME:_____

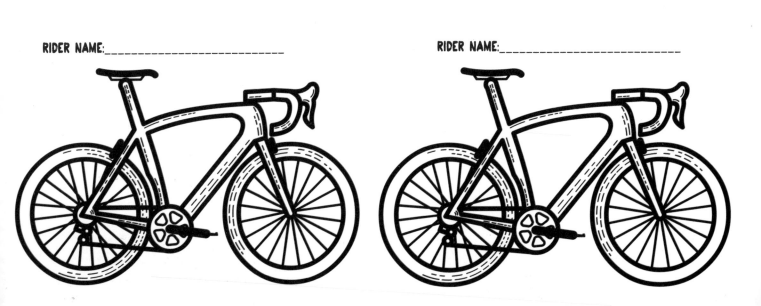

RIDER NAME:_____

RIDER NAME:_____

RIDER NAME:_____

RIDER NAME:_____

RIDER NAME:_____

RIDER NAME:_____

IT'S THE LAST GRAND TOUR OF THE
SEASON AND YOU WANT THE RIDERS
TO FEEL LIKE THEY'RE ON FRESH
BIKES TO PUT A SPRING IN THEIR
LEGS! COLOUR THE BIKES IN A NEW
BOLD PAINT JOB! GO FOR IT!

RIDER NAME:_____

DESIGN THE JERSEY

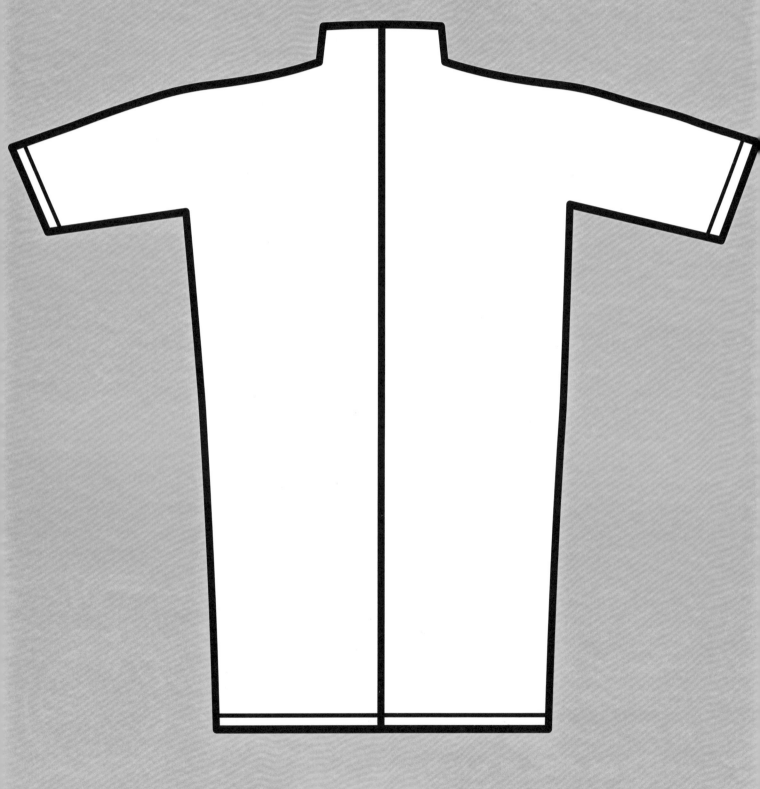

2010s

THE 2011 VUELTA A ESPAÑA

ROUTE BOOK

STAGE 18

SOLARES

NOJA

PUERTO DE BRAGUIA

ALTO DEL CARACOL

PUERTO DE ALISAS

PUERTO DE FUENTE LAS VARAS

174.6KM

THE GROUP FORMED EARLY AND THIS SETS THE TONE FOR THE STAGE. AFTER SOME SERIOUS DAYS IN THE MOUNTAINS THE PELOTON SEEM HAPPY TO LET THE GROUP GO UP THE ROAD AND SOON A GAP OF AROUND 10 MINUTES IS REACHED. WITH RIDERS LIKE JOAQUIM RODRIGUEZ, ROBERT KISERLOVSKI AND EVENTUAL STAGE WINNER FRANCESCO GAVAZZI IN THE GROUP THIS STAGE HAS SOME REAL RACERS IN IT TO REALLY LIGHT IT UP. IT'S GOING TO GET EXCITING TOWARDS NOJA, AND GAVAZZI PROVES IT WITH A FINAL ATTACK FOR THE LINE AND THE STAGE WIN.

WHERE WERE YOU THAT DAY? DID YOU MAKE THE BREAK? DID ANY OF YOUR TEAM MATES MAKE THE BREAK WITH YOU? HOW WAS IT RACING ALONGSIDE SOME OF THE MOST EXCITING RACERS OF THEIR GENORATION. THEY KNOW HOW TO GET INTO A BREAK AND MAKE IT STICK ALL THE WAY TO THE LINE.

WRITE YOUR ACCOUNT OF THE DAY ON THE NEXT PAGE, ADD IN LOTS OF DETAILS. IT'S UP TO YOU!

IT'S TIME TO PIN ON YOUR NUMBER. EVERY PRO RIDER HAS HIS OR HER OWN WAY OF DOING IT. DRAW THE NUMBER, WITH YOUR NAME ON IT, ON THE BACK OF YOUR JERSEY AND THEN ARRANGE YOUR PINS. DON'T LET THAT NUMBER FLAP!

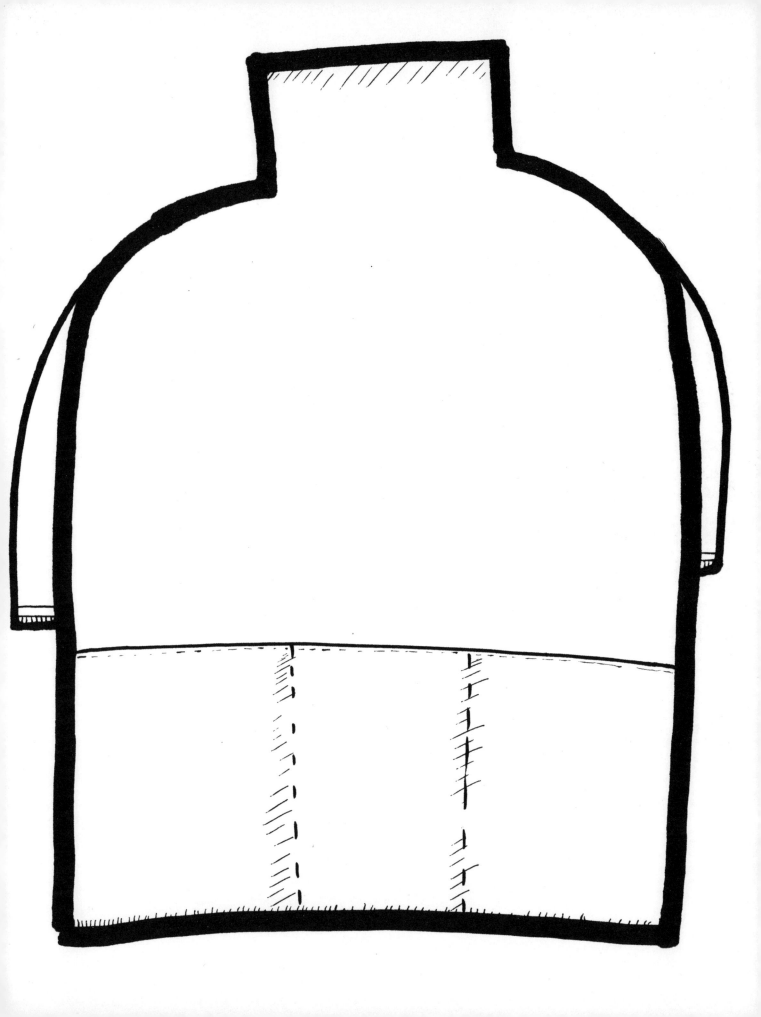

ALL THE RIDERS ARE UP FOR THIS. YOU CAN SHOW TO THE OTHER TEAMS JUST HOW STRONG YOU ARE AS A UNIT. YOUR SPRINTER IS CALLING THE SHOTS AND YOU ALL KNOW EXACTLY WHERE TO BE AND WHEN. COLOUR THEM IN. MAKE SURE TO HIGHLIGHT YOUR TEAM LEADER – THEY SHOW OFF THE WORLD CHAMPS BANDS ON THEIR ARM AND COLLAR AFTER THAT STUNNING WIN A FEW YEARS AGO. IT'S A BIG DAY FOR THE TEAM.

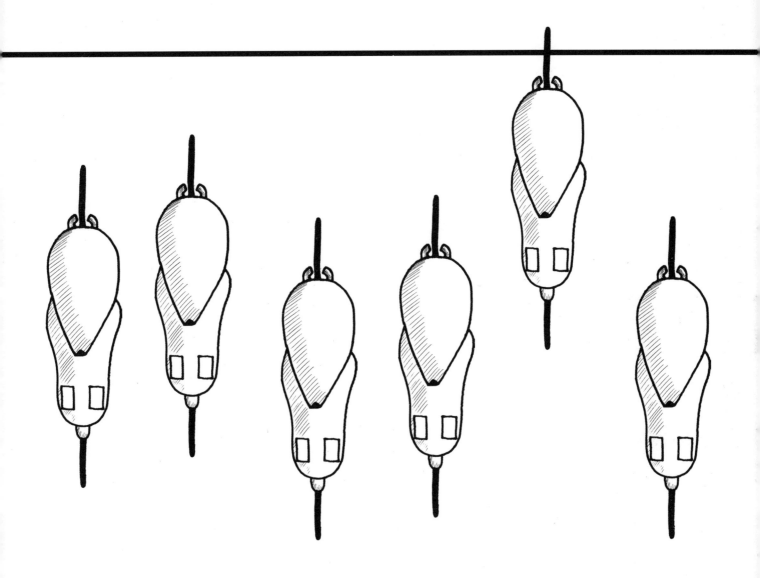

YOU'VE MADE IT, AND THE TIME LOOKS GOOD! YOU ROAR ACROSS THE LINE AS ONE. WHO DID THE TEAM DECIDE TO GO OVER THE LINE FIRST AND TAKE THE RED JERSEY? IT'S UP TO YOU! A BRILLIANT RIDE BY YOU AND THE WHOLE TEAM. THAT'S HOW YOU TEAM TIME TRIAL!

MEANWHILE... ON THE ANGLIRU

OUR FAN IS FIRST HERE! BUT I DON'T THINK THEY MIND THE WAIT. THEY ONLY LIVE DOWN IN THE VALLEY AND THEY'VE BROUGHT AS MUCH BEER AS THEY COULD CARRY. BUT THE REST OF SPAIN IS COMING TO WATCH THE RACE! DRAW THEM IN AND FILL BOTH PAGES ON THE INCREDIBLY STEEP ANGLIRU!

L'AMERICAIN

SOME OF GREG LEMOND'S MAJOR WINS:

GRAND TOURS

GIRO D'ITALIA
1 INDIVIDUAL STAGE (1986)

TOUR DE FRANCE
GENERAL CLASSIFICATION (1986, 1989, 1990)
YOUNG RIDER CLASSIFICATION (1984)
COMBINATION CLASSIFICATION (1985, 1986)
5 INDIVIDUAL STAGES

DOT TO DOT

STAGE RACES

CIRCUIT DE LA SARTHE (1980)

COORS CLASSIC (1981, 1985)

TOUR DE L'AVENIR (1982)

CRITÉRIUM DU DAUPHINÉ LIBÉRÉ (1983)

TOUR DUPONT (1992)

WORLD CHAMPIONSHIPS

GOLD MEDAL — 1983 — ALTENRHEIN

GOLD MEDAL — 1989 — CHAMBÉRY

SILVER MEDAL — 1982 — GOODWOOD

SILVER MEDAL — 1985 — GIAVERA DI MONTELLO

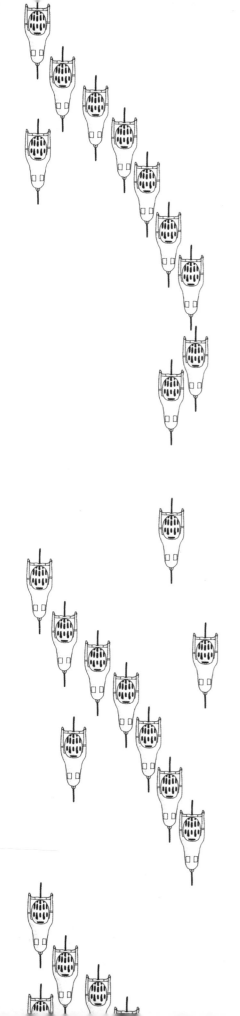

BANG!!!

WITHIN 2KMS BIG GAPS HAVE APPEARED. SUDDENLY EVERY TEAM LEADER HAS A VERY LOUD VOICE IN THEIR EAR TELLING THEM TO FIGHT, AND FIGHT HARD! IF THEY'RE NOT WITH THEIR RIVALS IN THAT FRONT ECHELON THEY CAN KISS GOODBYE TO STANDING ON THE TOP STEP OF THE PODIUM THIS YEAR.

WHERE IS YOUR TEAM? AND HAS YOUR LEADER MADE IT TO THE FRONT? IS IT TIME TO POWER ON AND MAKE TIME ON THOSE BEHIND? OR RALLY AROUND YOUR LEADER AND GET THEM BACK TO THE FRONT?

FAUSTO COPPI LEGEND.

THE RACE ROLLS THROUGH A SMALL VILLAGE. ALL OF THE PEOPLE THAT LIVE THERE HAVE TURNED OUT TO SHOUT, SCREAM, WAVE, AND WELCOME THE RIDERS TO THEIR PART OF THE WORLD. AN OLD LADY EVEN SHAKES HER PRIZED CHICKEN AT THE LEADER!

BUT, JUST AS THE MAYOR IS OPENING A BOTTLE OF THE LOCAL SPIRIT AT A JOB WELL DONE, A DOG RUNS OUT AND ONTO THE COURSE... HIS DOG! A MAJOR PILE-UP FOLLOWS AND THE WHOLE RACE STOPS!

DRAW THE RIDERS CRASHING AROUND THE OBLIVIOUS DOG. THE DOG IS FINE AND WALKS CALMLY AWAY. THE MAYOR REALISES HE WON'T BE VOTED IN AGAIN AND DRINKS THE WHOLE BOTTLE.

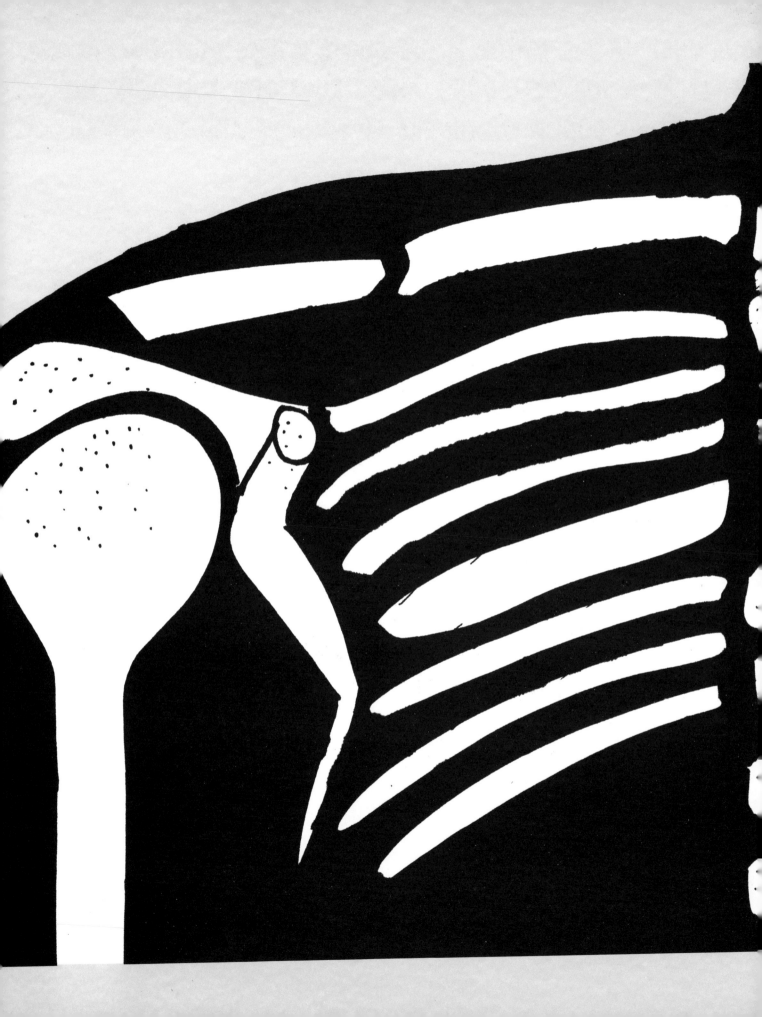

A DOG RAN OUT OF THE CROWD...

A SCREECH OF WHEELS, A CLATTER OF CARBON. SKY. GROUND. SKY. GROUND. PAIN... THAT WAS A BIG ONE, BUT YOU GOT TO THE END OF THE STAGE AND NOW YOU'RE IN THE HOSPITAL WITH A BROKEN COLLAR BONE.

PIN YOUR COLLAR BONE BACK TOGETHER. DRAW THE PINS IN. FIX IT GOOD.

REMEMBER THAT TEAM? AND THAT ONE? AND THE JERSEY THEY RACED IN? NOW'S YOUR CHANCE TO SHOW SOME REAL KNOWLEDGE OF CYCLING'S PAST BY COLOURING IN THE SQUARES IN THE COLOURS OF SOME OF THE MOST FAMOUS TEAMS FROM CYCLING'S PAST! TRY TO DO THIS FROM MEMORY!

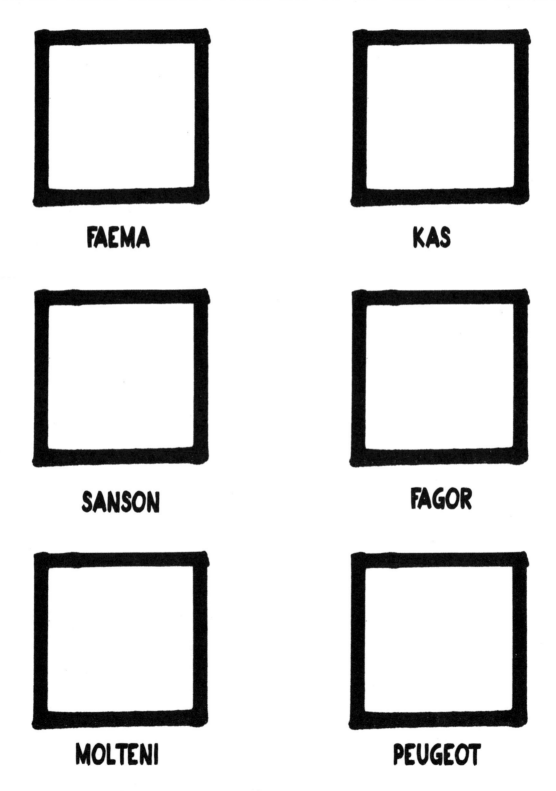

FAEMA

KAS

SANSON

FAGOR

MOLTENI

PEUGEOT

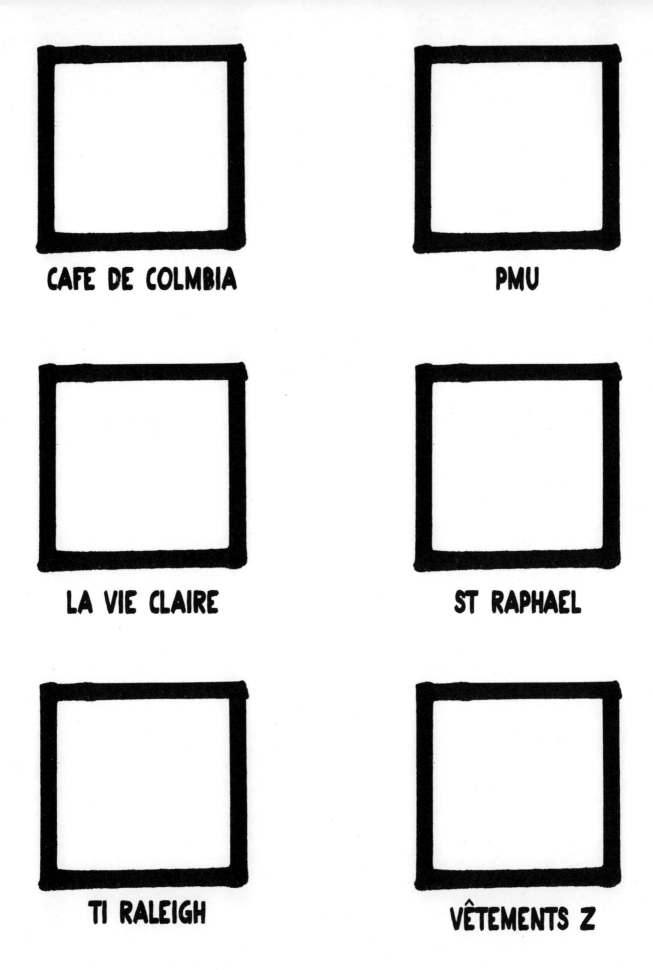

CAFE DE COLMBIA

PMU

LA VIE CLAIRE

ST RAPHAEL

TI RALEIGH

VÊTEMENTS Z

DRESS THE RIDER

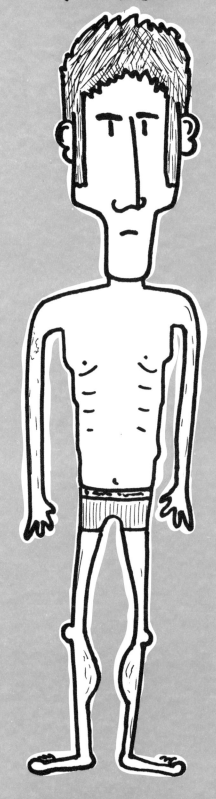

2010s

DRESS THE RIDER

2010s

MIGUELÓN

SOME OF MIGUEL INDURAIN'S MAJOR WINS:

GIRO D'ITALIA
GENERAL CLASSIFICATION (1992, 1993)
INTERGIRO CLASSIFICATION (1992)
4 INDIVIDUAL STAGES

TOUR DE FRANCE

GENERAL CLASSIFICATION (1991, 1992, 1993, 1994, 1995)
12 INDIVIDUAL STAGES (1989–1995)

WORLD CHAMPIONSHIPS

GOLD MEDAL 1995 DUITAMA
SILVER MEDAL 1993 OSLO
SILVER MEDAL 1995 DUITAMA
BRONZE MEDAL 1991 STUTTGART

THE DOT TO DOT

MARCO PANTANI
LEGEND.

GET YOUR THINKING CAP ON AND
DESIGN MARCO A NEW JERSEY.
THINK ABOUT THE TEAMS HE WAS PART OF
LIKE CARRERA JEANS, MERCATONE UNO.

THE BREAK FINALLY STUCK, BUT YOU'VE HAD TO TRY 3 TIMES AND YOUR LEGS ARE HEAVY AFTER THE EFFORT. THERE IS STILL 100KM OF TODAY'S STAGE LEFT, BUT AS NONE OF YOU FEATURE ON GC YOU'VE BEEN ALLOWED YOUR TIME IN THE SUN. A MOMENT TO SHOW OFF YOUR SPONSORS ON TV AND MAYBE, (PERHAPS) FIGHT IT OUT FOR THE WIN. THE BUNCH HAVE SEEN THIS AS A REST DAY SO YOU'VE TAKEN A RATHER IMPRESSIVE GAP. HOW BIG CAN IT GO? LET'S MAKE THE DAY COUNT. YOU CAN DO IT!

SOME CALL IT 'THE RACE OF TRUTH'. I THINK PEOPLE THAT ENJOY TIME TRIALS HAVE ALWAYS CALLED IT THAT. TODAY YOU'RE SUFFERING AND MAKING THE TIME CUT IS YOUR ONLY AIM... BUT THAT TIME IN THE WIND TUNNEL WORKED WONDERS. AND THE VOICE FROM THE CAR BEHIND IS PUSHING YOU ON. THE REST DAY IS TOMORROW. ON ON ON.

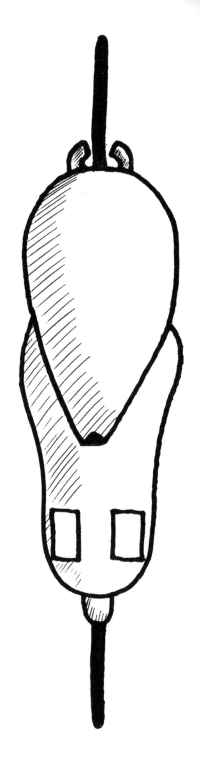

HOW HAVE YOU CAUGHT THE RIDER IN FRONT? PERHAPS THIS IS GOING BETTER THAN YOU THOUGHT IT MIGHT. THE VOICE BEHIND IS STILL PUSHING YOU ON. YOUR POWER METER STILL READS ON TARGET AND THE LEGS FEEL GOOD. MAKE SURE TO PUSH ON FROM THIS RIDER. DON'T LOOK. KEEP IN YOUR POSITION AND USE THEM AS A SPRINGBOARD TO THE FINISH. THIS IS A GOOD DAY. YOUR DAY.

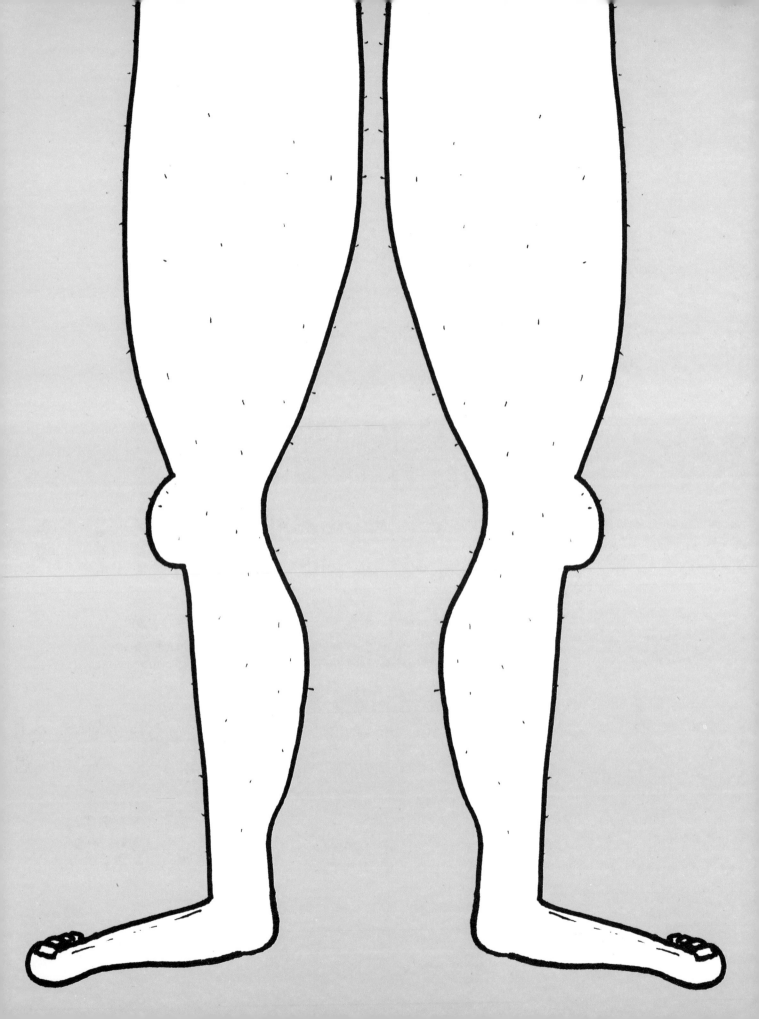

WHAT A LOVELY PAIR OF LEGS... THEY'VE HAD A HARD SUMMER'S RACING, AND IF WE'RE LOOKING CLOSELY COULD DO WITH A SHAVE... COLOUR IN THE LEGS AND SHOW YOUR TAN LINES FROM THE SUMMER.

THE REALLY BIG FAT WORLD OF CYCLING WORD SEARCH

P	K	I	D	B	S	E	P	H	F	G	P	I	N	K
W	O	J	N	I	O	A	D	C	X	L	J	P	C	O
C	M	B	O	D	H	E	A	N	E	C	A	R	M	J
H	E	B	M	O	R	R	A	U	B	O	T	T	L	E
A	P	O	E	N	B	N	K	B	I	Y	E	C	O	T
I	A	N	L	O	Q	A	A	C	A	G	N	R	I	G
N	T	K	N	U	U	E	H	W	A	E	Q	A	R	R
H	É	F	E	T	S	I	A	T	O	T	B	N	A	U
X	O	T	O	P	N	K	S	P	F	I	T	K	G	P
I	I	B	O	A	A	O	R	E	A	K	W	A	E	P
L	U	I	U	E	E	O	C	L	I	M	B	E	R	E
S	R	L	R	C	U	E	L	C	Y	C	I	B	G	T
U	T	B	O	T	T	O	M	B	R	A	C	K	E	T
M	U	S	E	T	T	E	C	N	E	D	A	C	Y	Q
B	L	O	W	U	P	E	C	H	E	L	O	N	I	Q

AERO	ANQUETIL	DIRECTEUR SPORTIF
ATTACK	LEMOND	DOMESTIQUE
AUTO BUS	HINAULT	ECHELON
BOTTLE	INDURAIN	ESPOIR
BIDON	BICYCLE	ÉTAPE
BONK	RACE	FALSE FLAT
BLOW UP	STAGE	GRUPPETTO
BREAK AWAY	MOUNTAIN	MUSETTE
BOTTOM BRACKET	FLAT	NEO PRO
BUNCH	SPRINT	PROLOGUE
PELOTON	KOM	SERVICE COURSE
CADENCE	YELLOW	SOIGNEUR
CHAIN	PINK	STAGIAIRE
CLIMBER	RED	STICKY BOTTLE
ROULEUR	POLKADOTS	TEMPO
PUNCTURE	LANTERN ROUGE	TIFOSI
CRANK	CARBON	VELODROME
DERAILLEUR	STEEL	GREGARIO

FIND ALL THE WORDS AND FEEL LIKE THE BIGGEST FAN EVER!

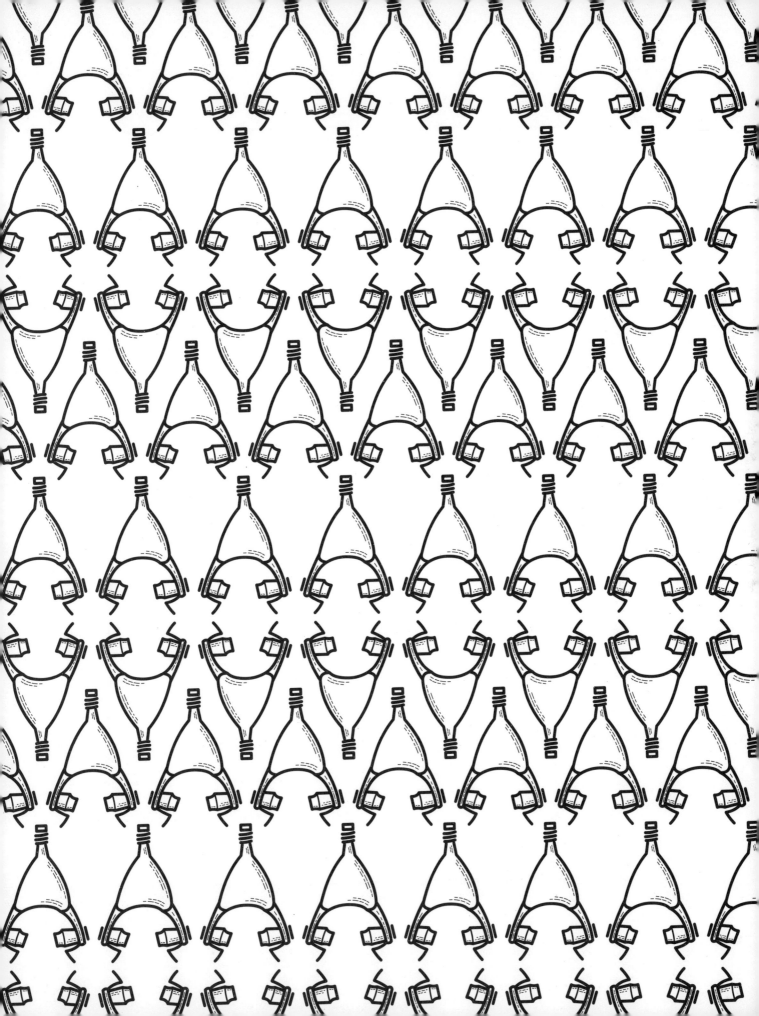

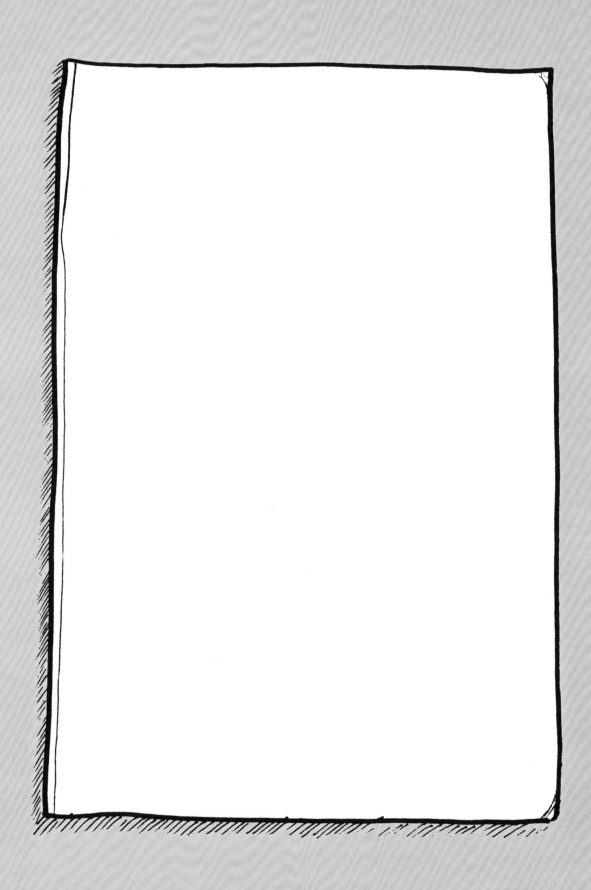

IT'S BEEN A TRULY MEMORABLE SEASON. YOU AND THE TEAM HAVE ACHIEVED GREAT THINGS AT SOME OF THE BIGGEST RACES IN THE WORLD. THIS IS THE FRONT COVER OF YOUR NEW BOOK. WHAT'S THE TITLE? WHAT PICTURE SITS ON THE FRONT? MAKE IT MEMORABLE. DON'T LET IT GO IN THE BARGAIN BIN AFTER A MONTH OR TWO.

YOUR TOP TEN RACES...

1. _____

2. _____

3. _____

4. _____

5. _____

6. _____

7. _____

8. _____

9. _____

10. _____